T0073611

Code for What?

Code for What?

Computer Science for Storytelling
and Social Justice

Clifford Lee and Elisabeth Soep

foreword by Christopher Emdin

epilogue by Kyra Kyles

The MIT Press

Cambridge, Massachusetts | London, England

The MIT Press would like to thank the anonymous peer reviewers who provided comments on drafts of this book. The generous work of academic experts is essential for establishing the authority and quality of our publications. We acknowledge with gratitude the contributions of these otherwise uncredited readers.

This book was set in Stone Serif and Stone Sans by Westchester Publishing Services. Printed and bound in the United States of America.

Library of Congress Cataloging-in-Publication Data

Names: Lee, Clifford (Clifford H.), author. | Soep, Elisabeth, author. | Emdin, Christopher, writer of foreword. | Kyles, Kyra, writer of afterword.
Title: Code for what? : computer science for storytelling and social justice / Clifford Lee and Elisabeth Soep ; foreword by Christopher Emdin ; epilogue by Kyra Kyles.
Description: Cambridge, Massachusetts : The MIT Press, [2022] | Includes bibliographical references and index.
Identifiers: LCCN 2022001970 (print) | LCCN 2022001971 (ebook) | ISBN 9780262047456 (hardcover) | ISBN 9780262371834 (epub) | ISBN 9780262371841 (pdf)
Subjects: LCSH: Computer science—Study and teaching—Social aspects—United States. | Computer programming—Study and teaching—Social aspects—United States. | Computer literacy—United States. | Critical pedagogy—United States. | Interdisciplinary approach in education—United States. | Social justice and education—United States.
Classification: LCC QA76.27 .L429 2022 (print) | LCC QA76.27 (ebook) | DDC 004.071—dc23/eng/20220521
LC record available at https://lccn.loc.gov/2022001970
LC ebook record available at https://lccn.loc.gov/2022001971

10   9   8   7   6   5   4   3   2   1

To our creative, grounded, artistic, hilarious, intrepid team of dedicated colleagues, of all ages, who are committed to sharing their brilliance and centering the voices of young people in all of our stories.

Contents

Foreword

Chris Emdin

In an era when teaching technology and computer science (CS) in schools has quickly grown from an indicator of innovative teaching to a new means of rehashing age-old pedagogies, the need for a new approach to engaging the next generation in CS is more necessary than ever. CS education is a relatively new, burgeoning, and innovative discipline. It is centered on new methods, consistently advancing technology, and a certain responsiveness to the world that teaching in most academic disciplines does not consider. This is why, for decades, the teaching of CS existed outside of the school day. Coding was almost exclusively taught in after-school and weekend programs and most instructors were not credentialed teachers or employees of school systems. It was this grassroots movement that sought to bridge the gap between the world of technology and young people that significantly shifted the relationship between schools and CS. Youths responded positively to the "coding academy" movement and schools began to support the argument that CS is necessary to prepare the next generation for an increasingly digital world. As CS has been brought into the school day in K-12 schools, however, there has been a challenge. Formal education is trying to shrink a broad and expansive new area of study into a rigid and unyielding school system that forces just about anything that is welcomed in to acquiesce to its traditions. CS then becomes a new example of how to make an important thing that is designed to live outside of the structure function to reinforce and replicate it.

CS is as much about form as function. It is both theoretical and practical and requires those who work within it to pull from a number of disciplines in order to make sense of whatever is being worked on. In schools today, despite overwhelming evidence that indicates it does not work for students, subjects are mainly taught in isolation from each other. Interdisciplinarity is still frowned on, assessments are still more focused on memorization than demonstration of deep knowledge, and instruction still anchors itself on what the adult in front of the room says instead of how the youths in the classroom make connections between what is shared in the classroom and the world beyond. For CS education to move forward in ways that reflect the field and not the school's version of it, we must acknowledge that innovative disciplines cannot coexist with antiquated pedagogies. Furthermore, pedagogical innovation (which is necessary to teach young folks to code or engage in other aligned tasks/goals) is about what we teach and how we teach it. If we teach coding as though it were a set of mundane tasks to be completed and do not capture the heart and imagination of young people, then we may as well keep teaching traditional academic subjects that do not prepare young people for an increasingly digital society. Teaching computer science in a hyperstandardized, overly technical, and decontextualized way (as it currently looks in most schools) extracts the beauty, joy, and discovery from learning and has serious implications on how young people are prepared for the digital world beyond the classroom that has increasingly become an extension of everyday life.

Code for What? is anchored in recognition of the points I have laid out above and concurrently centers the fact that we live in a world where the lines between the digital and the nondigital are irreversibly blurred. Online worlds that were once reserved for those with specialized technical knowledge or who work in technology-related fields are now accessible to almost everyone. Still, as digital worlds have become more accessible, they have not necessarily become more democratic. With the rise of social media, new economies, digital learning platforms, and even online forms of leisure, there is a narrative set in place that *all* people can fully participate online and in technology. This narrative exists under a desire for a digital utopia that allows those who participate in the current inequity to avoid facing the dystopic realities of far too many in present society. Those who work in technology have attempted to frame online worlds and the work/professions in those worlds as a digital escape from all that plagues our "real" worlds only to find that we inevitably replicate and exacerbate the ugliness of the real world when we don't work to address inequities in technology access, use, and exposure.

This book is a radical reimagining of STEM and an opportunity to see what people are doing to disrupt the status quo and demystify disciplines that have for far too long only been working for those with access and power. This is a reminder that at its core, technology is about making things that work for us. This concept of "working for us" is a fascinating one. We work for institutions, corporations, and organizations that do not work for us. We send children to work hard in schools that do not work for them. We toil to ensure that the systems we work for—their ideas, their infrastructure, and even their inequities—are maintained. Yet, there is no parity in what these systems give back to us. There is no mutualism in the relationship. That must be interrupted. That interruption begins when young people can name what they need and demand what work they want done for them. In this book, Clifford Lee and Elisabeth Soep provide superb examples of this happening in practice. When this interruption happens, we demystify STEM and science, technology, engineering, and mathematics become employees of the people. These disciplines now become tools to help us understand, design, and build a world that challenges the dystopia of the everyday and positions young people as the experts and professionals.

I am reminded here of one of my favorite quotes from aerospace engineer and inventor Lonnie Johnson, shared in my 2021 book *STEM, STEAM, Make, Dream: Reimagining the Culture of Science, Technology, Engineering, and Mathematics*, which says, "In engineering and technology, every kid can turn pro."[1]

This concept of going pro in technology and making the tech work for you is about centering the self, whoever the self is, in and through technology. It is about being queer and then using technology to advocate for queer rights, being socioeconomically disadvantaged and being able to discover the reasons for those conditions while learning financial literacy online. It is about the radical notion that one can center one's own history and truth when it has been pushed to the margins and use technology as the chief tool for this centering. It is also about being a professional/expert in who you are and having the ability to present a version of yourself that reflects what I call a ratchetdemic identity—a sense and vision of self that reflects both the ratchet (raw, expressive, unrepentant core identity) and academic self. In a world where young people are currently being inundated with images of themselves that are other people's perceptions of them, their sense of self has been so shaped by society that even their dreams are manipulated by reductive images from across the media. To counteract this and to create the conditions that allow them to be professionals at being themselves, the educator's duty is to show them images of what they can make themselves to be.

To make yourself into someone or something greater than what the world projects onto you is no small feat. In a society where narratives about marginalized groups have become a digitally curated and globally distributed vulgar pastiche of their truth, presenting who you truly are beyond the narratives is a revolutionary act. In fact, being oneself and operating as a professional at oneself is more innovative than any technology tool or platform. In an increasingly technological world where social norms are dictated by algorithms and even someone's interests are presented to them through the images placed across the screens they carry, the most innovative thing anyone can do is be themself. This type of innovation occurs when people have the courage to take risks, and a large part of that courage comes from being comfortable with reinventing, reimagining, and repurposing. The teaching of technology, computer science, or related disciplines must be about this type of innovation first. It is only when young people can innovate in their own lives that they can exhibit these same habits of mind with technology. The stories and backgrounds of many tech gurus sound similar. The privilege they have been afforded to be themselves in school or at home or in a middle class neighborhood has given them the permission to be innovative in their work in technology. They have given themselves the power to play and experiment. There is less emphasis on "doing it right" or "being perfect." They understand that there is no right way to be creative, and there is no failure in trying new things—other than not trying at all. When students learn how to fail forward—to learn from their mistakes as they find and form themselves, rather than getting discouraged and giving up—they build new forms of resilience that will help them fight for what they and their communities need to be well.

There is an unfortunate and false notion that some people are just born more creative, brilliant, or resilient than others. Young people walk into schools on the conveyor belt that is K-12 education and get marked as either having or lacking these attributes based on their proximity to institutional definitions that fail to see them for the geniuses they are. The reality is that none of those traits is some special gift that's bestowed on a select few. They are built into all children and are fortified by experiences and learning opportunities that allow them to be the ones that question, research, investigate, and participate fully in the world that is, so that they can use the tools at their disposal to create the world as it should be.

1
Introduction

There is no way the twenty-five or so teenagers crowding the second floor of YR Media's Oakland, California, headquarters are going to fit around the small table where editorial meetings happen. And there are only so many of the fancy office chairs—the ones that roll and spin—to go around. So most of the young people who've just arrived from nearby schools by foot, bus, or subway settle for folding chairs, or a wall to lean on. Having completed six months of free media production classes, members of this group earned their place and are paid to be here. As interns in YR Media's newsroom, interactive, and design departments, they're expected to represent their expertise and show up ready to make stories together.

The fashion is a mix of urban, athletic, vintage, punk, school uniform, and everything in between. Several of the young people play with gender in expansive ways, and there are plenty of bold style statements like fuchsia eye shadow, dyed-green hair, intricate braids, and acrylic nails shaped into points and studded with gems.

It's about as racially diverse a group as you can get—a range that is rarely reflected in the students' academic classrooms. The building is steps from various public transportation options—bus and subway—making it accessible to neighborhoods across Oakland. The six months of after-school classes that students take before they're eligible to be paid are free. At YR Media, you might find a teen struggling in school collaborating on a video or audio segment with a peer on the path to an elite college. Eighty-five percent of the young people at the organization are Black, Indigenous, People of Color (BIPOC), and most attend public schools with high percentages of students contending with material poverty. Beyond the young people involved in YR Media through its Oakland program, an additional three-hundred-plus teens and young adults participate via the organization's national network. Contributors access YR Media's open-source learning tools and workshops online, and they produce digital media for our own site and social channels as well as outlets including the *New York Times*, *Washington Post*, *Teen Vogue*, PopSugar, Radiotopia, National Public Radio (NPR), and local commercial and public radio stations nationwide.

As the young people stash their backpacks and drop into seats, they greet each other and banter back and forth. Also scattered around the room on this particular afternoon are five adult producers in their twenties and thirties who've previously worked in various newsrooms, tech companies, schools, and community health and youth organizations. Eventually Teresa, a former science teacher turned journalist in her thirties who's mixed race (Asian American and white), calls the room to attention.

> Today we're going to brainstorm some story ideas across our three departments. Each group should have a mix of different members. By the end of our brainstorm, each group will pitch their stories on their posters. Be sure to explain what kind of interactive you would add to your story!

Adult staff and youth interns take turns presenting five ideas for brainstorming. Immediately hands shoot up as young people volunteer for the various small groups, each of which finds a separate space to work. They have forty-five minutes to come up with a unique angle on a story and present a pitch for how to make it interactive. The options include a mobile app, game, quiz, map, data visualization, clickable infographic, or some combination that best brings audiences into the narrative experience.

This scene is typical of the first phase of ideation for any interactive project at YR Media. No matter what the youth team members make in the end, they will need to develop their skills in research and reporting, data collection and analysis, design and graphics, narrative storytelling, and coding to produce a digital product that communities will engage with online as well as share with their networks. At least that's the hope.

I (Cliff) sit with a group focused on gentrification, joining a small group of young people and one adult staffer. Yonas is a senior in high school, and Kendrick is a recent graduate attending community college. Ike is a newsroom producer.[1] Yonas, who is Black, and Kendrick, who is Latinx, have especially strong connections to West Oakland, the East Bay neighborhood closest to San Francisco's burgeoning tech industry where displacement is painfully pronounced. Both grew up there. Ike, who's Sri Lankan American, is a recent transplant to Oakland from a public media job in Boston. "Have the changes in your community benefited you or others?" Ike asks. Kendrick is the first to respond,

> I actually looked at the [crime] statistics in the West Oakland neighborhood. [It] hasn't even gone down that much, but it is definitely a step in the right direction. But [for] people who are there, it doesn't benefit them because they're financially segregated to East Oakland, or they're getting kicked out because they're either forced to sell their house or they cannot afford to live there anymore because the market price is really high. . . . These private corporations are coming in and real estate agents are coming in, and they're just buying up the whole place!

The dynamics that Kendrick describes began in the 1990s and intensified after the 2008 recession. Between 1990 and 2011, the Black population in West Oakland dropped from 77 to 53 percent.[2] Large companies purchased hundreds of foreclosed homes at far below market rates and flipped them into investment rentals.[3] Kendrick has noticed the imprint of these developments on the architecture of his neighborhood—like a brick building that was recently purchased.

"Yeah, they painted a mural on it. I think within like three or four months. . . . They basically made new apartments. The thing is . . . great, you have these new people who are coming in, but they're not contributing to the community at all whatsoever."

"All the people who have moved in within the last couple of years, I still haven't spoken to," Yonas says.

"Right! Yeah!" chimes in Kendrick.

"My family and I consider ourselves neighborly people," Yonas goes on.

"Like our neighbors across the street, our neighbors a couple doors down, we talk to all the time. But it's not the same with the people who are coming in."

Kendrick remembers the lively Sunday football and soccer games he used to join at the park near the building. "I can tell you firsthand, the Latino community from West Oakland comes all the way together there. They also interact with the African American community. But you don't really see . . . I hate saying this, but people who are Caucasian. You don't see them there at all. They're basically becoming the majority in our neighborhood."

The ease with which Kendrick and Yonas dive into this conversation is not uncommon at YR Media. They readily share research, personal experiences, and theories about barriers to community connection.

You may be asking, though, What does a discussion like this have to do with the focus of this book, *Code for What?* It's a fair question. The young people are not engaged in processes we typically classify as computational thinking. And yet for us, to practice computer science (CS) in the fullest sense is to understand, on a deep level, the lived experiences of the makers and users of the technology we create, and act on that understanding in pursuit of justice. One tool for that action is code. Exploring a community's complex histories along with the current cultural and political dynamics is too often seen as, at best, a positive if time allows. An extra. At YR Media, that work is foundational, nonnegotiable, and ongoing. Young people's critical insights are interwoven through every aspect of product development—not a separate and distinct "user research" phase that translates into a slide or two in a presentation deck, but a lens on the entire process that centers the voices, strengths, rights, and needs of systemically underserved communities.[4]

From CS for All! To Code for What?

From the moment we wake up and scroll through news headlines on our phones during breakfast, to the last heart we hit on a friend's post before bed, most of us are chronically connected to technology. You may even be reading this book on a phone, tablet, or laptop. And if you're holding a physical copy in your hands, we'd venture to guess that you're probably within arm's reach of a mobile device.

Given the explosion of technological tools and the computational power necessary to run them over the past two decades, it comes as no surprise that the educational sector that propels this growth is surging too.[5] The push to teach CS has been taken up by politicians, nonprofit leaders, school district superintendents, CEOs, and even professional athletes and musicians. Many of the initial US proponents framed their arguments along economic and equity lines.[6] They made the case for democratizing computing for women as well as Black and Brown students so that they are equipped to sustain our global competitiveness and advantage. "In the coming years, we should build on that progress, by . . . offering every student the hands-on computer science and math classes that make them job ready on day one," President Barack Obama declared in his 2016 State of the Union address. Highlighting the digital divide and participation gaps, Obama's commitment and related efforts around the country accelerated the proliferation of local organizations, district projects, and national movements to make CS part of the core curriculum.[7]

In 2021, New York City school chancellor Richard A. Carranza announced an $81 million private-public partnership to ensure that "all NYC public school students receive high-quality CS instruction in elementary, middle, and high school by 2025."[8] Advocates pointed to second graders introducing coding to their kindergarten peers, lunch and code sessions, and combining yoga and coding as examples of what was implemented.[9] A major highlight during CS Education Week in 2021 was the Hour of Code, a global challenge to spend one hour learning programming basics through tutorials and activities.[10] The event engaged more than 1.2 billion people in more than 180 countries, according to the initiative's website.

Like our colleagues who have worked to broaden participation in CS education over the last decade, we, too, are passionate about bringing the voices, perspectives, and experiences of historically marginalized communities into tech. Our own teaching in schools, nonprofit organizations, and grassroots advocacy efforts is indebted to their foundational work. That said, we believe that if CS education fails to prepare students to explore ethics or recognize technology's role in reproducing inequality, the default setting will be to replicate a system with inexcusably small numbers of Black, Latinx, and Indigenous people, materially unprivileged groups, and women in positions of full participation and leadership. We have found some of the early dominant approaches to diversifying tech to be paradoxically limited—overly hopeful, on one hand, and not audacious enough, on the other.

On the overly hopeful side, there is this underlying notion that young people who are underrepresented in tech only need the right CS skills to find success and transform how the sector operates. The logic goes something like this: if we "train" girls, Black and Brown youths, and those living in material poverty with programming classes or boot camp–style programs after school, professional opportunity will greet them on the other side. Moreover, once members of underserved communities move into tech jobs, we'll start to see major improvements in the kinds of tools and platforms their employers make, thanks to a freshly diversified workforce that better reflects the United States.

That sounds reasonable—and yet it doesn't work. Imagine a fresh-out-of-college engineer who is, say, Latinx, and/or from a very small town, and/or one of only a handful of girls who graduated from her university with a CS degree. She shows up for work at a start-up or tech giant, and we expect her to not only thrive individually but also transform the culture? Should it be her responsibility, and is it even reasonable to imagine that she can change the system and structure from within by her mere presence? Recent diversity hiring efforts by tech companies have resulted in troubling headlines describing outright sexist and racist workplace conditions.[11] As gender equity researcher Kimberly Scott said in her keynote address at a National Science Foundation meeting of informal educators in 2017, to set young people up for tech jobs without addressing the hostility in those environments amounts to a form of child abuse.

Now what makes "code for all" not audacious enough? Education efforts designed to democratize participation in walled-off fields like science, technology, engineering, and mathematics (STEM) tend to reduce learning to the basics in order to make these disciplines more "accessible." While global movements like CS Education Week and Hour of Code are great at drumming up the initial excitement for novices and young learners, what happens when the work moves beyond aesthetically pleasing, gamified, block-based coding with instant video game–like results? How will these students sustain the passion, motivation, and resilience necessary when faced with the inevitable error message? How do they see themselves as well as their communities and culture within their code? What is the appeal for those who are grappling with sociopolitical struggles, and are driven to produce technology that allows them to express their full selves while shifting conditions that have held them and their communities back?[12]

What's at Stake

Over the past decade and a half, we've seen significant efforts to repackage CS education by adding culturally relevant framings, aesthetics, and perspectives. These can be worthy developments. But what 2020 showed us is that tacked-on popular culture references and kid-friendly graphics are not enough. The global pandemic and subsequent shelter-in-place orders forced many of us to take stock of what is truly important in our lives, such as health, family, spirituality, creativity, values, and purpose. The national and global reckoning with anti-Black racism after the police killings of George Floyd and Breonna Taylor further exposed white supremacy as not a fringe relic of the past but instead a force that continues to contaminate and threaten our present and future—and one that technology can fuel and make worse. The near-daily violent assaults on Asian American elders and uptick in racism targeting the whole community during the pandemic revealed the vicious danger of online hate, especially when amplified by twice-impeached former president Donald Trump and others in positions of power.

Rather than adding cultural frames to our curricular and pedagogical approaches in a superficial way, we're interested in fundamentally reconfiguring our learning ecologies. Schools and other learning spaces provide an opportunity to build the world we want. To do that, we've got to ask the big questions. What do we teach? Why are we teaching it? What persistent inequalities might we be perpetuating? In what ways do we serve some students and harm others? How can our lessons be truly liberatory for all learners?

In the United States, our education system underfunds majority-BIPOC schools with a turnstile rotation of novice teachers and administrators, while bespoke tax policies and parent, teacher, and student association funding prop up wealthy schools.[13] Schools are increasingly segregated by race and class, and embrace curriculum and standards that cater to white, middle-class values, content, skills, learning, and communication styles.[14] So the outcomes we see today shouldn't surprise us. The shift to online classes in the pandemic only shined a light on these glaring inequalities: disparities in access to computer hardware and software for students and teachers, unreliable broadband access, unequal resources and training for teachers, and a lack of basic social and economic support for our most marginalized students and their communities.

We have an opportunity to reimagine as well as reinvent CS education by framing coding as a storytelling medium and computational thinking as a resource for justice.[15] Instead of narrowly focusing on technical skills, we can center the real-world issues that young people are passionate about—creating the kinds of relevant lessons they want from their teachers and schools. Students in a CS class might spend periods of time not even touching a computer. They might share their own stories and delve into youth-centered issues with sociopolitical awareness.[16] They might explore how the state has long used surveillance technologies to police and control BIPOC communities, from enslavers' patrols to border checkpoints to stop-and-frisk law enforcement practices.[17] From there, young people might engage in an ideation process, sharing their own and their families' experiences with state monitoring, and starting to form ideas for what new story they want to tell through a combination of research, narrative, design, and code. They might conduct interviews, collect data, develop wireframes and user flows, create art assets, and program an interactive web-based experience or mobile app that allows users to interrogate a present-day instance of surveillance society. Their message might be troubling, but often young people will find playful and creatively stunning ways to deliver sobering stories. They might develop features that convey humor, irony, artistry, and imagination without compromising their critique. These are the kinds of rich learning experiences that describe what CS education can be.

Why Now?

Computational thinking has the potential to extend into experiences of civic insight, community connection, accountability, creative expression, and hope. In our work at YR Media, we push ourselves to break the arbitrary boundaries that tell young people "science is this, not that." We see the world as fundamentally interdisciplinary and young people as having a "rightful presence" in whatever field they want to practice.[18] If we want to create transformative digital tools and platforms, we must work to undo the structural inequities that marginalized people face and create nourishing learning spaces where they can create with liberatory aspirations. We have an opportunity to set young people on pathways not only into the technology sector but also fields where we need their critical talents—media, design, urban planning, education, organizing and activism, economics, and electoral politics.

We feel an acute sense of urgency to shift thinking on CS education right now as a growing cadre of technologists, ethicists, journalists, scholars, and policy makers is sounding alarms about the impact of unbridled growth in digital and computational technology.[19] In prior eras, it could take decades or the better part of a century for new technology to become ubiquitous. Nowadays, world-bending innovations like personal computers, smartphones, and social media platforms powered by artificial intelligence (AI) land in our homes and hands much more quickly. Because these inventions happen so fast and often come in black boxes, humans don't have time to adjust and evolve with the technology, or create the learning opportunities, policies, and safeguards we need.[20] What has humanity gained and lost in this process of technological "advancement"? How are these tools shaping the human psyche, behaviors, actions, relationships, and society in ways that were not intended, nor do we want? How have corporate technology behemoths leveraged decades of psychological research to shape our decision-making in ways that increase their profit margin? What happens when our brains can't match the processing speeds of our devices?

The results of this unchecked hyperexpansion is evident in the effects of biases rampant in the technologies that we use and that use us. In her book *Automating Inequality: How High-Tech Tools Profile, Police, and Punish the Poor*, Virginia Eubanks reveals how public services that automate decision-making can hurt low-income and working class people in the United States. From Indiana's privatized welfare system that wiped out benefits that a million people depended on, to the use of algorithms to determine who among the unhoused deserved shelter in Los Angeles or who was likely to commit child abuse in Pittsburgh, Eubanks shows us what happens when we remove vital human judgment from large, complex systems in the name of efficiency and cost cutting.[21]

In related research on algorithmic bias, University of California at Los Angeles (UCLA) professor Safiya Umoja Noble Googled "Black girls," and found sexually explicit terms and images as the top results, whereas her search for "white girls" resulted in mostly positive, wholesome attributes. Noble's findings reveal the ways in which big tech's search engines can create, maintain, and disseminate racism and sexism.[22] Researchers Joy Buolamwini and Timnit Gebru exposed the extent to which facial recognition systems discriminate against women and people of color. They found that darker-skinned women were the most misclassified group, with error rates up to 34.7 percent, as compared to a maximum error rate for lighter-skinned males at 0.8 percent.[23]

To grasp the damage these biases produce, we have to look no further than the case of Robert Julian-Borchak Williams, the first-known person to be wrongfully arrested based on facial recognition technologies.[24] Each new headline like the Williams case points to the profound human cost of seemingly technical shortcomings like inaccurate and unethical predictive algorithms, flawed facial recognition software, problematic risk models, and automated eligibility tools. Taken together, these systems make up what Ruha Benjamin calls "the New Jim Code," the interconnected and mutually reinforcing technologies "that reflect and reproduce existing inequities but that are promoted and perceived as more objective or progressive than the discriminatory systems of a previous era."[25] The New Jim Code is sneaky and insidious. It presents itself as neutral, if not benevolent, while doing great harm.

Despite this sobering backdrop, the ten years' worth of work we highlight in this book is full of hope and promise. We honor the amazing ways that technology can be leveraged for good: accessing food, transportation, and communication tools for people living with disabilities; instantaneous information and resources in the immediate aftermath of natural disasters; the use of AI to detect contamination in public water supplies; and even bots that provide everyday supports grounded in techniques of cognitive behavioral therapy. Likewise we take inspiration from artists' use of technology in general and coding in particular as instruments of expression. If we didn't believe in the potential of CS as a means to unlock opportunities, hold power accountable, and express creativity, we would spend our time trying to keep young people *away* from tech rather than organize and investigate learning environments that enable them to produce it. Fundamentally *Code for What?* questions how technology shapes humanity and vice versa. It's not a question we'll ever fully answer, and yet we've found it endlessly generative—on practical, political, and conceptual levels—to keep asking.

What Do We Mean by Code?

Let's take a moment here to unpack the term *code*. In the context of CS, code is the set of instructions that programmers produce for computers to execute. Coding is just one dimension of CS, and those working to broaden participation in the field have gone to great lengths to make that case—which is important. Within CS, coding is the activity that often gets the most attention and credit for supplying "the magic that turns ideas into products."[26] But in the context of, say, the curriculum for Advanced Placement CS classes, programming is just one of five big ideas. The others are creative development, data, computer systems, networks, and the impact of computing. We strongly agree that an expansive view of CS is what will draw the youth talent that the field needs to produce excellent and ethical technology. So why, in this book, are we leaning into code?

The appeal for us probably reflects our training in the social sciences and humanities. In the intellectual and cultural traditions that have shaped our approach, code is the opposite of a narrow concept. We think of codes as systems of words, letters, numbers, signs, or symbols that are used to represent something else. Consider genetic codes, Mayan codes, building codes, codes of ethics, honor codes, secret codes, barcodes, coded language, and code-switching. In her book *Other People's Children*, Lisa Delpit—an education scholar who has influenced both of us in profound ways—builds an entire framework for understanding how schools fail Black children based on her concept of tacit "codes of power."[27] For us, codes open up worlds of meaning that help us grapple with the sociocultural implications of what and how we make with technology.

Take, for example, a company's code of conduct. On the face of it, a conduct code outlines how employees are supposed to act based on an agreed-on set of rules, responsibilities, and norms. But on a deeper level, these guidelines adjudicate what it means to *be professional*—and by contrast, what behaviors violate that standard. Consider just one aspect of a code of conduct in traditional US corporate workplaces: attire. This single guideline, often tossed off in a phrase like "business casual" that assumes a shared understanding of what that means, can smuggle in all sorts of cultural assumptions. And codes do not only operate explicitly. Tacit interpretations of what options are in or out of bounds leave plenty of room for discretion that can be either inviting or exclusionary depending on the context. In a workplace where business casual translates to button-down shirts, polos, blouses, khakis, knee-length skirts, and dress shoes, at what point do garments or jewelry that express a person's cultural, ethnic, or gender identity push the limit or cross the line? What about hairstyles, makeup, pins, and statements printed on T-shirts? Who decides? How are the guidelines set and expressed, both out loud and in unspoken ways? Beyond the intentions of the code's creators, what are its effects on employee equity, recruitment, retention, and well-being? These are the kinds of questions we ask of tech-based learning environments including our own.[28] We have found the double meaning of code, taken literally and metaphorically, to be a useful way to invite the level of inquiry that the situation demands.

This expansive view of code helps us to see computer programming in a new light. With every apparently technical decision they make, programmers are also making "implicit and explicit choices about the purpose, framing, and scope" of the products they're developing.[29] If we do not contend with the values and motivations of the programmers and software companies that guide as well as profit from their code, we cannot fully understand how these ubiquitous tools shape our lives. This is not a book taking aim at the outsized power of a single CEO at the helm of a giant multinational corporation pulling levers that strip us of our humanity. We are much more interested in the millions of rank-and-file designers and developers distributed across teams, companies, countries, and continents who make moment-to-moment decisions that can start to feel like "givens"—just "the way things work." We probe the assumptions behind what we take for granted as high-quality code, both the mechanics of it and the cultures that produce it. This critical work takes on even greater urgency in light of the capacity for AI to replace programmers with algorithms that evolve as the machine "learns," reflecting and in some cases worsening the bias of the humans who designed these systems. To fulfill the promise of broadening participation in CS, we need to examine the codes that shape our digital lives, and create pathways that diversify not only who writes the code but also how the learning and work environments it springs from function, based on what values, and serving what social ends.[30]

So when we ask, "Code for what?" we are interrogating the intentions behind the push to teach coding for all. We are asking about the underlying ideologies that drive these codes, and the planned and unforeseen effects. As the documentaries *Social Dilemma* and *Coded Bias* reveal, even industry titans who've designed some of our most popular social media features and artificially intelligent tools admit that they cannot anticipate the impacts of their inventions on humans or society, let alone predict how machine learning will evolve over time. We can't make these predictions either, and that is why we do our best to interrogate the potential impacts of our own products, messages they deliver, and ways we can hold ourselves accountable to the individuals and groups we align with. In short, we center code in our approach because of its fluid and flexible meanings within and beyond CS, and as a reminder to ourselves to always examine the process behind the products we program, and the implications of our technical choices on social life now and into the future.

Where We Work: YR Media

While coding exists in the digital sphere, most of our work takes place in shared physical space with young people (that is, before and after the global pandemic sent us into lockdown). The twenty-thousand-foot brick building that houses that work sits on the corner of two busy streets in downtown Oakland, just a couple subway stops from the West Oakland neighborhood that the youth team was talking about in that brainstorming session that opened our story. Chinatown is a short free shuttle ride away. Lake Merritt is close enough that if they really want to, YR Media staffers can get there and back on a lunch break. Four miles from the building is the Fruitvale Bay Area Rapid Transit Station in East Oakland where on New Year's Day 2009, an unarmed Black father named Oscar Grant was restrained facedown on the ground of the platform, and then shot and killed by white transit officer Johannes Mehserle. You'll see murals honoring Grant's life all throughout Oakland including, at one point, on YR Media's own building.

Art is on display everywhere in Oakland's public spaces, in murals like these, the distinctive architecture of its neighborhoods, street fashion, and events like the annual Life is Living Festival as well as Pride, Chinese New Year, and Black Joy parades. Public statements of political solidarity are everywhere too, frequently expressed through marches that almost always pass right by the front doors of YR Media, where an illuminated ticker broadcasts headlines across the building's third floor and an exuberant painting of two young people of color, one wearing a they/them T-shirt and with a fist lifted in the air, stretches across three stories.

That ideation session that we opened with, where young people were just getting started on a gentrification project that would take more than a year to complete, unfolded on the building's second floor, home to YR Media's multimedia newsroom. The teens and young adults who staff the newsroom produce features and investigations, opinion pieces, interviews, and first-person essays using video, audio, photo, illustration, the written word, and of course, web-based and mobile interactive projects like the ones we'll focus on for much of this book.

Next door to the main YR Media space is a second location that houses the music department, where young people work with professional producers to create beats, soundtracks, playlists, albums, and graphics. Also part of the music department is All Day Play, YR Media's one-of-a-kind 24–7 streaming radio station.

Upstairs from the newsroom is a floor for administrative staff and, crucially, wraparound services. YR Media provides academic and career supports to young people, and case management services including assistance with basic life needs and mental health counseling. There's a kitchen and open area for gathering in the basement. This space is usually where young people head first when they arrive after school to help themselves to fresh food—vermicelli noodles, chicken quesadillas, mac and cheese, or seasonal salad—before starting class or clocking into work.

If you were to visit YR Media in the middle of the day, the space would be fairly quiet, apart from the occasional muted bass thumping through the gap between the walls and ceiling of the street-side studio on the first floor where All Day Play DJs spin their sets. Come 4:00 p.m., it won't be quiet anymore. Teens and young adults stroll, rush, or amble in, individually or in pairs or groups, under headphones or else in midconversation. They'll stop to say "hi" to Patrice, who runs our reception area, and log into the front desk iPad. Most have probably stopped noticing the wall they walk past that's lined with shelves holding some of the most prestigious honors in journalism and media: George Foster Peabody, Robert F. Kennedy, Edward R. Murrow awards, and so on. Among the shiny metal statues and wooden plaques, there's a photo of a YR Media leader and student standing with then first lady Michelle Obama for an honor the organization picked up from the White House in 2012.

The building's first floor is where media education classes are held, taught mostly by recent program graduates who are now peer educators, supported by an adult faculty member who brings media and youth development expertise. For the first three months, teens between the ages of fourteen to eighteen rotate through a series of roles that all contribute to a Friday night radio show streamed from another street-side studio that neighbors the All Day Play sound booth. In addition to hands-on media production, a critical media literacy curriculum rounds out this introductory course, recently updated to account for the impact of machine learning on how we produce, consume, and share truths and lies. After this first course, students graduate to a second, more advanced one. For the next three months, they specialize in the field they're most interested in: news, music, or multimedia. By the end of the session, they'll have created a collaborative final project of some kind, at which point they become eligible to apply for paid internships across every department of YR Media. Some choose the music team, newsroom, video, or the design department. Peer education is always a popular internship. Especially the more outgoing students appreciate getting to move so quickly from newbie to teacher status, mentoring and educating students who could be the same age as they are, if not a little older.

The department where we'll spend most of our time is what we call interactive, where young people combine journalism, design, data, and coding to create content that defies static, one-way publishing. By definition, the products of the interactive team engage audiences, and we mean this literally. The makers design web-based and mobile experiences that invite users to join the narrative by clicking, swiping, or otherwise navigating through these experiences, which mix visuals, quantitative data, and words. Sometimes the designs call on users to take further action—such as respond to questions, use a drawing tool, operate a slider, or pick from a set of options—to determine what happens next in the story. Developing these products is what requires the computational know-how that we have learned to teach and tried to capture in our model explored in *Code for What?*

As far as we know, YR Media's interactive department is the only youth coding program in the United States that is embedded in an award-winning national newsroom, and it's hard to overstate the impact of this dynamic. When "computer science for all" began to emerge as a rallying cry, most of the programming that followed took place in formal CS classes inside schools or in after-school opportunities that aimed to prepare young people for jobs in software development at start-ups or big tech companies. We absolutely and systematically work to prepare young people for higher education and jobs. Opening these kinds of pathways was one of the interactive department's founding values, as conveyed by its cofounder, Asha Richardson:

> YR Media is centered in the tech hub of the world. And technology has a lot of different career paths. But technology is one of the main driving economic factors of financial stability. And I think it is critical, no matter what it is that you're passionate about as a young person, to know that you could—you don't have to, but you could—be in one of these high salary positions that fuels your area, that changes your area, that ultimately creates technology that changes the world.

Within this context, YR Media's home base in an organization that has always and will forever be dedicated to justice-oriented storytelling has both forced and allowed us to approach CS education in our own way. We frame code as an expressive medium through which to carry out the work that journalism and creative media do best: amplifying community voices, exposing wrongdoing, holding officials accountable, moving audiences, and documenting history in the very moments that we make it.

Why Us?

YR Media was founded in 1993 under a different name, Youth Radio. Homicide rates in Oakland were spiking at the time, and public media journalist Ellin O'Leary was covering the story. Troubled by the dehumanizing reporting she was seeing in mainstream publications and broadcast outlets, O'Leary saw an opportunity to fill a gap by producing first-person radio commentaries with the young people most affected by the violence, and who were closest to the counternarratives missing from the public record.[31] Once those original youth team members got started down the path of producing their own stories, they didn't want to stop. And they wanted to add music to the program options. Without a sizable budget or nonprofit status initially, the founding group had no choice but to take on teaching responsibilities for new students and help invent the model. This is how peer education and youth leadership became core values that defined the organization's earliest phase, and continue to guide how we work today.

Lissa

Sometime around 1998, I was driving across the Bay Bridge, which connects San Francisco to the East Bay neighborhoods of Oakland, Berkeley, and Richmond. A story came on the radio from a young woman reporting on her decision to follow in her dad's footsteps by taking a job with the US Postal Service. It was a great piece. At the end, she signed off with the line, "From Youth Radio, I'm Jacinda Abcarian, in Berkeley, California." I was a student at Stanford's Graduate School of Education at the time, closing in on my PhD, and was experiencing some pretty serious ambivalence about life as a university-based scholar. I'd worked as a producer on a documentary so had some media experience, and my dissertation was all about community-based youth media programs. I had only discovered NPR a few years earlier, when a roommate told me about the interview show *Fresh Air*, which played nonstop at the lab where she worked. I'd quickly become a devoted public radio listener and felt drawn to journalism as a field where maybe I could do some of the same things I loved about academic research, but in a way that reached a broader public and wouldn't require a university library to access. So when I realized that the nonprofit where Abcarian produced that story was just across the bridge from my home in San Francisco, I called up the place to see if I could volunteer.

After a series of interviews with young people and staffers at the organization's one-floor rental space in Berkeley, where YR operated at the time, I started teaching writing two afternoons a week while finishing my dissertation. That's all it took. Collaborating with young people on stories full of characters, scenes, sound effects, and scoring; witnessing, learning from, and helping to support their creative processes; listening alongside them as we turned up the volume when their story aired on NPR for audiences in the tens of millions—it's what I wanted to do. As a white woman in a majority-BIPOC space, I was keenly aware of the generosity of my colleagues and students, allowing me to find a place for myself in this rich, creative, challenging community. I graduated, turned down a tenure-track job, and figured out a role at YR where I'd essentially trade the skills I'd acquired in graduate school, supporting the organization's efforts to formalize its curriculum, in return for the opportunity made possible by colleagues including Beverly Mire, Rebecca Martin, Anita Johnson, and Whiz Ward II to learn journalism on the job, alongside my students.

Fast-forward almost exactly ten years. By this point YR had grown large enough to fill our four-story building in downtown Oakland. Maybe it was something about living in the Bay Area, where it felt like a new tech start-up appeared each week somewhere in the neighborhoods between Silicon Valley and San Francisco's south-of-Market districts where I lived. Maybe it was my involvement with the MacArthur Foundation's Digital Media and Learning research, looking into the effects of what we called "new media" on youth literacy and civics. I started to sense an opportunity for YR. I sensed it was time for us to move beyond partnering with young people using existing digital tools and publishing our work on the available platforms. Young people needed to be the ones designing and developing those tools and platforms on their terms. This was also around the time when mobile tech was opening up new opportunities for media producers to serve communities in personal and dynamic ways through interfaces customized for phones.

Enter Asha, a YR graduate raised in Oakland who had started with the organization as a high school student, and had reported a handful of thoughtful national stories about digital media and technology, from identity theft on MySpace to a lack of diversity in tech. She'd moved on to enroll in nearby Mills College, and when YR got a grant to begin experimenting with some kind of mobile play, I remembered Asha's astute insights about the role of technology in young people's lives. So I reached out. "Oh, we're going to do something different?" Asha remembered thinking when I pitched the idea that she come onboard. "I was like, yeah, I'm down, I'm down to do this."

Together we formulated a pilot: to develop a mobile app that we could package alongside YR's more conventional coverage of the economy, which in 2009 was in the middle of a recession. The app we made never took off. Yet the idea for building a program to make more of them did. In 2010, Asha and I officially cofounded what we called the Mobile Action Lab. On the merits of a pitch that Asha delivered in our submission to a MacArthur

Foundation global competition, we got funding for the program, followed that same year by a National Science Foundation grant to partner with MIT. For the first few years, we focused on making downloadable mobile apps. "We were making it up as we go," Asha recalled about the early days, back when we were working with just two high schoolers who were our first students. Our model was based on storytelling from the start. "We know how to outline a story," Asha said. "So let's think about this app as if it's a story, with a beginning, a middle, and an end for what we want the person to do. Let's make an outline." We worked like that for awhile and at some point realized, "Oh wait, this is called UX!" Initially we experimented with relying on outside tech experts to run workshops. "But a lot of people we were working with didn't have really any experience working with young people. Definitely not a lot of experience working with Black and Brown young people from Oakland, from the Bay Area," Asha said. "And I was like, you know, maybe I can take this and lead in this space. Maybe I could help inform how we take all of these learnings and package them into something that could be a lesson, or repro-ducible and also fun."

With that, Asha took the lead in running the program even as we created it. Over time we've iterated on the model to align with YR's unique expertise: justice-oriented storytelling reaching real audiences. We renamed the department interactive and created the foundation for what is discussed in this book, *Code for What?*

It strikes me now that while Asha's technology and business expertise outstripped mine from day one, and played a major role in setting up our fledgling program for growth, we had something important in common: both of us came from the arts. For high school, Asha went to Oakland School for the Arts, where she concentrated in photography. I had spent my childhood and teen years strongly identified as a visual artist, and in fact among the most definitive experiences in my own education was the summer I spent at age fifteen in an arts program that was a lot like YR. There I made friends with a multiracial, diversely talented, experimental, and unafraid group of artists who showed me the kind of creative, politically engaged life that was possible beyond the conventional values of my suburban public high school outside Hartford, Connecticut. Other colleagues we eventually brought onto the interactive team as the program grew shared this deep connection to the arts. And that helps explain why we together designed an approach that foregrounds technology's expressive qualities and aims to expand points of entry into CS.

Cliff

As immigrants from Hong Kong and latchkey kids growing up in the suburbs of the Bay Area in the 1980s and 1990s, my sister and I had a lot of independent time from our continually hustling, working parents. I spent countless hours sorting, organizing, and reading my baseball cards and comic books, and watching cartoons, sitcom reruns, and cable TV. My indoctrination to US culture came from *Growing Pains*, *The Jeffersons*, *Punky Brewster*, and *Family Matters* as well as *Yo! MTV Raps*, *120 Minutes*, and *Headbanger's Ball*. In retrospect, I had surprisingly diverse tastes in music as an elementary school–age kid. Our family also spent a good portion of its free time watching US movies, trading the latest multiple-part Hong Kong television shows with friends, and making the occasional visit to check out the latest hyped movie from Hong Kong at the Great Star theater in San Francisco's Chinatown. Our family even got *Prodigy*, one of the first online platforms, and my friends and I learned to use dial-up bulletin board systems, which powered my many multihour video game binges. In high school, I used different friends' camcorders to make silly short films, and every chance we got, we would create hilarious-to-us videos for school projects.

So it shouldn't come as a big surprise that when I reflect back on some of my fondest memories of my seven years as an English and history teacher at Life Academy, a public school in the flatlands of East Oakland, many involved youths and media, creative expression, and technology. I remember toprocking, six-stepping, and doing freezes with my students and coteachers in a breaking cipher as a final showcase of our hip-hop intersession class. We ran around Oakland, Berkeley, San Francisco, and the greater Bay Area capturing on-the-street interviews and B-roll for students' group film projects for our documentary filmmaking class. On exhibition night at our school, my colleague and I shared our eleventh graders' US immigration digital story projects that described family members' journeys to the United States, many of which involved traumatic and harrowing border crossings. Crowded in a classroom fit for thirty-five, nearly a hundred family and community members watched as their own perilous journeys come to life. Through sobs and tears, they saw their histories legitimized by their kids' school in the form of family photos, maps, and their own children's narration. This was 2005, a peak of the national scapegoating and criminalizing of undocumented immigrants. These experiences taught me the power and potential of the creative arts and storytelling, especially when the stakes are high, work is public, and content is personal.

Five years later, as a graduate student and budding researcher in Los Angeles, I introduced my tenth grade class of CS students to *Ayiti*, a video game that entrusts players to help the Guinard family navigate the harsh realities of rural life in Haiti.[32] Facing scenarios based on real-life events, most players have a hard time keeping all five members alive for the duration of the four-year period. For twenty minutes, my students were transfixed by the game, reacting audibly during play, and expressing shock, frustration, anger, and empathy during our subsequent debrief. I left that day awed by the potential for games and other immersive, interactive digital products to engage learners as well as cultivate compassion for people and global issues that seemed so distant.

As I reflect on my past, media, creative expression, storytelling, technology, and justice have always been a part of my life. So when a former classmate shared an email about a four- to six-month, part-time opportunity to join Youth Radio as the scholar-in-residence, I was curious. The email had the following descriptors:

"Community-based, youth-driven organization."

Yes! I thought to myself.

"A researcher to study the activities of a dynamic team of young people creating media stories and mobile apps . . . and create dynamic new storytelling tools and platforms."

Seriously? Was this written for me?

"Work with Oakland youths"?

Okay, I was in after the second line. Where do I sign up?

Mind you, this was only eight months after my post-doc and dissertation, for which I had spent three years working with the Exploring Computer Science team in Los Angeles public schools to develop culturally relevant curriculum and pedagogy.[33] My own dissertation had examined the affordances of creating a choose-your-own-adventure Scratch video game with high school youths about an issue important to them and their communities.[34] It also laid the foundation for the framework we've developed in this book through a concept I called *critical computational literacy*.[35] That four-month stop turned into a life-altering seven years at YR Media.

A final turning point in YR's history is key to understanding the story of this book. In 2018, we officially changed our name from Youth Radio to YR Media, signaling a fundamental shift in strategy that reconstituted the organization as a national network of primarily BIPOC teen and young adult journalists and artists from across the United States. The organization had at times asserted its journalistic credibility through association with legacy media partners like NPR, where we served as the official youth desk. As YR Media, we would continue to produce for major outlets, but now we did so while investing in our independent, owned-and-operated online platform. With this new strategy, youth contributors could truly shape the content they wanted to create to engage audiences of their peers. In February 2020, Kyra Kyles, media veteran and leading voice for newsroom diversity, equity, inclusion, and excellence, joined the organization as the CEO to steer YR Media into the future.

What's to Come

In the following chapters, we will answer the question in our title, *Code for What?*, through five responses that we generated from our research and hands-on collaborations with young people. What do we code for? We code for insight, connection and community, accountability, creative expression, hope, and joy. Each chapter begins with a narrative, much like the opening scene of this one, and we keep returning to moments of making throughout these pages. Our stories interweave quotes from youth and adult collaborators, transcripts of recorded conversations as teams wrestle with key decisions, retrospective reflections with makers and other stakeholders, and ideation drawings, wireframes, and screenshots of our products at various stages of completion. Across the five themes, we consider twelve interactive projects that YR Media's interactive team has created over seven years. Young people have explored gendered and racialized dress code policies in schools; designed tools for LBGTQ+ youths experiencing discrimination; investigated facial recognition software and what you can do about it; recast a street in their neighborhood through illustrations of what it looks like now and how it could be; and developed a mobile app using original graphics and relevant language to promote mental health through self-awareness and outreach for support.

Our final chapter highlights how others have taken up what we call *critical computational expression* and applied it in a range of settings, from college classrooms to online communities to art and science museums. Collaborators we know and others we hope to work with someday are evolving the framework, and inspiring us to keep retooling how and what we produce with young people as well as how we make sense of what we're learning. The work continues.

2
A Framework: Critical Computational Expression

To gain clarity on how we think about our world, first we have to understand how our experiences and underlying ideologies shape the way we see it. In academic discourse, conceptual frameworks provide us with the language and a lens to understand our research. They supply mental maps or visual organizers for ideas. And they orient our present and future selves: how to think, what to say, how to act, and how to make sense of whatever we encounter.

Over more than a decade, the two of us have independently developed our own conceptual frameworks based on our respective teaching, learning, and research spaces. Lissa's thinking is anchored in her practice at YR Media, and collaboration with academic thought partners and coalitions, including the Youth and Participatory Politics research team she was a part of for seven years, its affiliated network on Connected Learning, the Civic Imagination Lab at the University of Southern California, and the Science Learning Plus initiative.[1] Cliff's educational praxis was sharpened with his students and colleagues at Life Academy high school, where equity, justice, and community sat alongside interdisciplinary project-based learning. His work as a teacher consultant with the Bay Area Writing Project, National Writing Project, and the Connected Learning initiative led him to forefront multiliteracy practices. The critical and sociocultural grounding he received from powerful UCLA mentors clarified his ideological stance while his Exploring Computer Science team concretized the work in curriculum and pedagogy all over Los Angeles public schools.[2]

For both of us, the ultimate point of all of our work has always been to support and advance collective movement toward social justice. Over the course of seven years, we've cocreated research agendas, youth programs, curricula, and digital media products in collaboration with dozens of YR Media staff along with close to one hundred young people. On the interactive team specifically over the period of time we span in the book, of the young people who self-identified by race, 40 percent were Black, 18 percent were mixed race, 15 percent were white, 13 percent were Asian American Pacific Islander, 13 percent were Latinx, and 2 percent were Middle Eastern. Their processes and products, together with ours, formed the basis for our conceptual and pedagogical framework of critical computational expression (CCE).

CCE integrates three domains of practice: critical pedagogy, computational thinking, and creative expression. With it, young people foster social action by producing and sharing interactive digital media. Through the community-responsive, transformative, interactive products they create, young people can reimagine what's possible in their lives and futures, and work with others to pursue that vision for change. CCE synthesizes vibrant traditions from the social sciences, STEM, and the arts, honoring the interdisciplinarity and deep humanity of a society that depends on, but cannot be reduced to, its near-constant use of technology.

Unpacking CCE

In their moment-to-moment interactions, the emerging reporters, designers, and developers at YR Media move within and across the three spheres of CCE through their real-time collaborative decision-making, shifting from one to the next, sometimes in a single line of argument. These are the kinds of moments we've found most instructive, and that you will observe again and again in the pages that follow. But first, let us briefly explore each sphere of CCE.

Critical Pedagogy

Critical pedagogy serves as a beacon and constant reminder of the role nonhierarchical teacher-student relationships can play for communities working to liberate

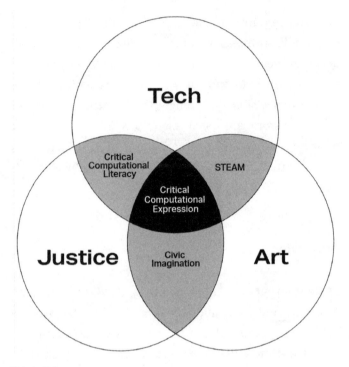

Figure 2.1
A visual diagram of the CCE framework.

themselves and one another by dismantling systems of injustice.[3] It rejects the traditional *banking model* of education, where the teacher deposits information into students' minds for them to receive, memorize, and store as if they were empty vessels. By contrast, critical pedagogy calls for a *problem-posing* education that encourages collective dialogue grounded in cycles of action, theory, and reflection—what educator Paolo Freire called *praxis*. The model insists that interrogating power and domination has to be at the center of education, directly addressed with students. Otherwise, these forces warp how we teach and learn, and diminish our humanity. Given the current state of schooling and global developments that tether us to devices, Freire's humanizing approach to education feels even more relevant now that systems of oppression materialize from algorithms operating the machines in our hands, and us too, if we let them.

Computational Thinking

While critical pedagogy gives us the perspective we need to grapple with the role of technology in society, computational thinking helps us to live with and produce algorithms in nuanced and empowered ways. As we have seen, the discipline of CS spans a wide range of topics well beyond coding. Underlying all of them is computational thinking: the process of breaking down problems into smaller parts, allowing us to recognize patterns, apply principles, and design procedures that can be carried out by computers to generate solutions.[4] The process reveals the fraught relationship between computers and humans: "What can humans do better than computers? What can computers do better than humans? What is computable?"[5] Our focus on computational thinking provides us with the flexibility to adjust our lessons depending on the activity at hand. At YR Media, we've developed interactives that involve a range of CS topics: human-computer interaction, algorithms, programming, data structures, science communications, machine learning, object and speech recognition, natural language processing, and more. Computational thinking is a lens that young people can apply to whatever project or problem they face, with growing nuance and sophistication as they advance in the work.

Creative Expression

Over the past three decades, the curriculum in US schools has narrowed to focus on a smaller and smaller subset of skills and subjects that students are expected to demonstrate proficiency in via standardized exams.[6] Opportunities for creative expression have shrunk dramatically. Stand-alone arts classes and interdisciplinary courses that integrate the arts are few and far between—more so than ever with pandemic-era learning barring students from studios and stages, assuming their schools ever had them. It's tempting to justify arts learning by pointing to its positive impact on academic grades, test scores, and other outcomes.[7] This tendency is especially strong in relation to science, as evident in debates over the framework of science, technology, engineering, the arts, and mathematics (STEAM). By wedging the arts among four academically dominant disciplines, STEAM runs the risk of valuing the arts only to the extent that they open doors to these other fields, thereby depleting the powerful learning experience of art making on its own terms.[8] In prioritizing creative expression as a key sphere of CCE, we don't disregard evidence that the arts can enhance attitudes toward learning and well-being, broadly defined.[9] But we are much more focused on arts learning as a way of knowing with its own characteristic practices, which honor traditions of making as well as expressing the self and culture rooted in marginalized communities, and foster habits of healthy risk-taking while aligning with efforts to advance social justice.[10] Also, in practical terms, young people want their interactive digital media to look and sound amazing. That won't happen without a dedicated focus on learning in and through the arts.

Glimpsing CCE

Our understanding of CCE takes inspiration from the robust examples we have encountered over the years that demonstrate the power of learning and making at the intersection of each possible pairing among our three spheres of practice.

Critical pedagogy + computational thinking: Native Land exemplifies this first pairing. This nonprofit based in Canada created a digital map showing Indigenous territories, languages, and treaties across the world.[11] Code for Anchorage utilized this resource to create an SMS bot that allows users to text a location and generate a corresponding statement acknowledging the historical lands of Indigenous communities.[12] Through projects like these, which deploy computational thinking to counter the devastation of settler colonialism and cultural erasure, makers exercise voice and power.

Computational thinking + creative expression: Projects that integrate tech and arts include creative code, programmable objects as art, e-textiles, DanceON, STEAM dance makerspace, hip-hop and CS, and Modkit.[13] They show us what is possible when youth learners are given the space to imagine, create, and collaborate with digital tools. These examples have the potential to multiply points of entry for learners into both CS and arts fields.

Critical pedagogy + creative expression: Multimedia initiatives including youth participatory action research, public arts projects, hip-hop expressions, critical arts pedagogies, and social justice art connect art to advocacy and activism.[14] "Civic imagination" is one framework that we've found especially useful as a way for young people to apply their most expansive creative thinking to their work toward building a better world.[15] While not necessarily tied to technology or digital media, these projects could easily incorporate computational thinking as another means to create and disseminate work.

Across these examples, even projects that favor two of CCE's tenets can extend across all three, and ambitious frameworks like *critical digital making*, which use programmable art objects to engage with sociocultural contexts, connect art, tech, and justice in ways from which we have a lot to learn.[16] One dimension of YR Media's context that adds a layer to these related efforts is our orientation toward the audience. Everything the interactive team creates is released to the public, often packaged with other content for distribution via platforms and social feeds reaching hundreds, thousands, and sometimes tens of millions of people. With this kind of distribution, young people can leverage their products of CCE to spark fresh local and national conversations about the most pressing issues affecting their lives, communities, and our shared social world.

From Theory to Practice: CCE as Method

The pedagogical foundations of our CCE framework stretch back over a century to the origins of progressive education, with the work of John Dewey. In his book *My Pedagogical Creed*, Dewey laid the groundwork for an experiential form of learning, where students solve problems as a means to grow.[17] The role of the teacher is to steer students to direct their own investigations and experiments, motivated by their interests, in and around their environments.

Maria Montessori, Jean Piaget, Lev Vygotsky, and Seymour Papert went on to expand these concepts, forming a basis for other constructivist and sociocultural learning theories.[18] Unlike the transmission-based model of teaching, constructivism recognizes and utilizes the full spectrum of knowledge and experiences that learners bring to the classroom. It holds that when we translate concepts into concrete products, we can accomplish more sophisticated tasks than when we operate only in the realm of abstraction. Learning along these lines challenges young people to explore real-world problems through ongoing, interdisciplinary projects investigating complex questions that hold genuine consequences for those involved.[19] Sociocultural theories add the collaborative dimension to this pedagogical approach, arguing that we learn together and from one another through "communities of practice."[20] Novices in these communities initially need a lot of support. Over time and with scaffolding, they move toward full involvement in meaningful collective activities, eventually building the capacity to work more independently and helping to draw in the next wave of newcomers.[21] This dynamic aptly describes the way we work on YR Media's interactive team.

In building a method to support this work, we are indebted to the model of youth participatory action research, which adds a nuanced understanding of power to our project-based orientation. This approach to research centers young people's knowledge and leadership—and not just any young people, but those directly affected by the disparities they explore and address.[22] Together with peers and mentors, the young people with the most at stake are best positioned "to develop solutions for social, cultural, and political transformation."[23] Young people, teachers, researchers, scholars, and community activists have used youth participatory action research to address issues including racial disparities, food instability, and inequitable school discipline policies.[24] Of late, proponents are adding emerging technologies (mobile devices, social media, mapping platforms, etc.) to the tool kit that young people can use to advance justice through investigation and the creative representation of their findings.[25] When young people combine their local knowledge with digital technologies and data analyses, they begin to see themselves as "community leaders and community builders who are connected and committed to [the] health and well-being of their neighborhoods."[26]

In order to achieve these outcomes, self-determination must be one of the stated goals for any project that centers the perspectives of the "multiply marginalized and dispossessed communities . . . into organized, socially transformative action and, as important, reflection on the activism as lessons to improve these processes for sharper analysis and critically compassionate practice moving forward."[27] Individual self-actualization alone is not enough, wrote bell hooks. "We must be linked to collective struggle, to communities of resistance that move outward into the world."[28]

Our education colleagues Jeff Duncan-Andrade and Ernest Morrell have developed a model for collaborative research that is grounded in youth communities as sites for collective resistance.[29] They partner with students to move through steps of identifying, investigating, and implementing a plan to address a problem, and then evaluating the efficacy of those actions in order to reassess the state of the problem and determine the necessary next moves. Crucially, young people's insights, resilience, and leadership shape every step along the way, from framing the inquiry to forming solutions. Research "rigor" in this context is judged based on the soundness of its design, methods, and results as well as its genuine accountability to communities with the most to gain and lose.

The steps for critical collaborative research that Duncan-Andrade and Morrell have laid out help us to put critical pedagogy into action. We have identified two additional sequences of steps that align with the remaining spheres of CCE: algorithmic problem-solving as a method for cultivating computational thinking, and artistic ways of knowing as a method for promoting youth creative expression (table 2.1 below).

For the purposes of laying out a method, we have found it helpful to visualize the parallel steps across these three pedagogical approaches in a linear way. Each moves through four phases that correspond to framing, planning, executing, and assessing an impact. But in reality, the process is messy. The nonlinear nature of the work is perhaps most evident with respect to framing. It's where the activity begins; it's the first step of identifying, naming, and defining a problem. But it's also the phase that never ends because the new information we take in through research, experimentation, and testing with our communities will invariably force us to go back and

Table 2.1

A Comparison of the Pedagogical Approaches of Critical Civic Research, Algorithmic Problem-Solving, and Artistic Ways of Knowing.

Critical praxis in research	Algorithmic problem-solving	Artistic ways of knowing	Contexts where the three come together
Partnering with young people from impacted communities who set the terms for collaborative investigations tied to social issues affecting them, with the goal of bringing about positive change. See Duncan-Andrade and Morrell, *The Art of Critical Pedagogy.*	An approach to understanding and solving problems through a set of step-by-step procedures following a logic that can be expressed in various ways including code. See CS Unplugged, www.csunplugged.org /en/.	A stance toward creating, perceiving, and interpreting arrangements of symbols (colors, lines, shapes, sounds, movements, and words) that are replete with meaning. See Mejias et al., "The Trouble with STEAM."	Learning environments where participants take on thorny topics and problems, and work together to produce media that offers solutions and drives new conversations, using a combination of investigative, technology-based, and artistic tools to achieve the impact they seek for themselves and their audiences. See YR Media, where young people collaborate with professional journalists, designers, and developers to create interactive digital content for online distribution and community engagement.

(continued)

Table 2.1
(continued)

Critical praxis in research	Algorithmic problem-solving	Artistic ways of knowing	Contexts where the three come together
Identify and research a problem from the points of view of those acutely affected.	Describe a problem in detail.	Frame a problem based on "deep noticing."	For a project on gentrification, young people share personal experiences and other forms of data (such as demographic shifts and housing patterns) to figure out what story they want to tell, and in what format—for example, a map populated with illustrations, audio, video, and text that connects West Oakland's proud past to its present and possible futures.
Develop a collective action plan to address the problem, accounting for diversity of experiences, especially those that have been historically and systematically overlooked.	Break the problem down into logical steps.	Define the approach, including materials, styles, and sign systems.	For a project on school desegregation, the youth team formalizes roles, and establishes a timeline and assignments for phases of design, production of media and graphic assets, coding, testing, community engagement, distribution, and digital afterlife. Each phase prioritizes equity and inclusion as a lens to inform decision-making.

| Implement the action plan. | Use these steps to solve the problem. | Apply artistic principles to materials using established and novel techniques. | For a project on bias in facial recognition systems, a youth team comes up with creative solutions to obstacles; for example, for a digital drawing tool that invites users to test how much they have to scribble over a face to dodge AI detection, the designers need to find an open source for faces that won't require users to compromise their privacy by uploading their own images. The producers identify a database of multiracial portraits generated by AI and program the interface to pull from that source. |
| Tap engaged communities to evaluate the efficacy and ethics of the action, including unintended outcomes, reexamining the problem, and broader implications on that basis. | Evaluate how well the solution works to inform updates to the product and broader opportunities for technology innovation. | Assess how well goals have been met, considering how the work reflects, challenges, and advances arts traditions. | For an app designed to promote social and emotional well-being by inviting users to track their feelings using emoji, the youth team holds a debrief with peers and experts to reflect on the process and product, brainstorm updates to the app, and identify takeaways related to the concept, user experience, visual and graphic design, and insights for youth mental health and well-being services through an equity lens, to inform future app-building projects as well as critical media stories and actions calling for change. |

revisit our working assumptions, in some cases dismantling a design and starting again.

The digital media we produce aims to make a positive difference in the world, reflect and sometimes even
advance best practices in online and mobile user experiences, convey their makers' imaginations, and deliver
on aesthetics.[30] Of course we don't hit the highest marks
across all of these aspirations with everything we make.
Sometimes we fall short or abandon a project we've been
working on for months. Stories of disappointment show
up throughout the book because we need to learn from
our failures alongside successes and support one another
in the effort. This work is challenging, but necessary, if
we are to reimagine what's possible not only in CS learning specifically but learning as a whole too. Learning that
is community connected, culturally relevant, enabled but
never defined by technology, tethered to truth, powered
by creative expression, and oriented toward justice.

3
We Code for Insight

Coding Gentrification, Revisited

Let's get back to Yonas, Kendrick, and the other designers who were getting started on an interactive project related to gentrification. When we left off, they were describing changes they had observed in West Oakland's people, rituals, and built environment that benefited some and harmed others. They were exploring various possible story lines that could become the basis of the digital product they would create.

"But what will be the interactive?" Ike asked, pushing the young people to get more concrete about the user experience they had in mind. By *interactive*, Ike means the digital interface that the creators would design to play out the story. What would users actually see when they arrived at the site? What actions could they take? What could they click on, slide, swipe, listen to, watch, look at, read, choose, or share? How would those options allow users to contribute their insights and navigate through the narrative based on their own interests?

With this kind of prompting, Ike is navigating the tricky balance between giving space for process and focusing attention on product. While free-form ideation has yielded some of our richest concepts, we have also learned the hard way that too much conceptualizing can leave us with insufficient time to build the thing we've imagined. We have definitely been guilty of analyzing and tearing apart every possible angle, perspective, or audience response until we've effectively hollowed out the project as well as killed the enthusiasm.

Conversely, there have been times when we have prematurely committed to a design, and missed important perspectives or overshot our own technical abilities to execute. On occasion, we've only realized what we were missing during a final testing phase days before the deadline and have had to make the tough call to undo hours of effort in order to address the late-stage realization of a design flaw. This experience is as painful as it is relatable to any producer working on complex digital projects.

It is against this backdrop that Ike steers the conversation toward a specific interactive product. Yonas proposes a map of West Oakland that reveals patterns of gentrification: "If you've got a map of West Oakland and you've got DeFremery Park here [gesturing to a blank space on the butcher paper], and you can look at somebody's recounting of how the block parties have disappeared. Every street or every landmark has a story." The idea immediately has something important going for it. It leverages a core competency of YR Media's newsroom: first-person narratives.

This is one of the ways our coding program stands out from other comparable CS curriculum, whether inside schools or through community-based initiatives. YR's interactive department is embedded inside a youth-driven newsroom. Designers and developers collaborate with content creators to deploy coding in service of telling a dynamic, interactive story. Narratives comprise some of the most powerful data around which we code.[1] Sometimes we relate to code *as* narrative—just another sign system through which to convey a community truth.

"There's been a lot more tearing down of houses. You know they tore down one of the houses where Huey P. Newton used to live?" Kendrick offers.

"No! Really?" Yonas says, incredulous.

"That was a historical landmark, and they just completely renovated [it]," Kendrick says. "It's crazy how even though they're historical landmarks, they just come in and completely just take it up. . . . It's like, 'Okay, you guys don't care about the historical value of this building.'"

"Or of anything in Oakland, apparently," a late arriving student adds.

Here Kendrick confronts a hypothetical person who's not literally in the conversation but whose presence nonetheless hovers—a person responsible for the troubling patterns of displacement that Kendrick has noticed in his community. He addresses that figure directly. This is just one of the ways that the points of view considered during the ideation phase of making an interactive expand beyond those physically present in the discussion. Creators embody various perspectives—even those they disagree with—as they refine their idea, and this act of imagination unlocks insights.

"Maybe it could be a map of West Oakland with these places that are—maybe not on an official map anywhere, but known by everybody in the neighborhood," Ike suggests, synthesizing the range of ideas he's heard so far. A map of important places at risk of being forgotten. With that, the team is definitely onto something.

Coding for Insight

Coding for insight builds toward moments like these of synthesis, understanding, and connection. When a group of designers comes up with a way to convey nuanced knowledge through an imaginative user experience, that's coding for insight. When designers collect and analyze data, and grapple to understand what it tells them. When a group discussion reveals the potential unintended consequences of a project in development and the participants rethink their approach as a result. When they face a technical limitation and problem solve around it. These are instances when insight is both a result of the development process and a resource to improve the product.

Coding for insight requires a willingness to take a fraught concept like gentrification, interrogate it, experiment with ways to tell an interactive story about it, create a visual design and creative assets to bring it to life, and then exercise the computational skills to code that story into existence. Coding for insight is nurturing the conditions for developers to deeply understand an issue in all of its complexity and how to represent it accurately, while being attuned to how users might make meaning from it. Journalists might call the products of coding for insight "explainers," and as interactive team members, we're in a position to produce especially dynamic ones because of the range of opportunities for user engagement we can build into the experience.

Often we think of insight as occurring in a flash, like a light bulb switching on, or that iconic moment in *Matrix* after Neo chooses the red pill. In this view, insight is contained within a person's mind and demarcates what that individual took to be true "before" versus "after." While this conventional understanding may capture what a revelatory moment can feel like, it obscures the experience of insight as a collaborative process that unfolds over time, and shifts as participants in a shared process continue to learn and create together.

What we see again and again at YR Media are the ways in which insights evolve, for makers and audiences. Insight shifts when we apprehend something about ourselves, such as how we were raised, the values we have internalized, or the taken-for-granted knowledge legitimized by our respective upbringings. It is revealed in layers, with each opportunity building on others, and instilling new understandings of ourselves, the world, and the things we create. We saw this earlier when Kendrick came to see the freshly minted mural on the refurbished apartment building in his neighborhood not as a feel-good attempt at "beautification" but rather as a front for false community connection.

A final thought on what we mean when we talk about insight in the context of coding. It is not just the creators' development that matters here. Ultimately an interactive like this one, about gentrification, aims to shift insights on the part of users as well. There are at least two steps involved in making that happen:

1. The producers need to understand enough about their target audience to get people engaging in the first place.
2. They need to create a digital experience that points those users toward the kinds of revelations the makers have in mind.

You'll see in the discussions through this chapter and others across the book that interactive producers constantly project and play out scenarios for how audiences will experience their digital stories, and what conclusions they'll draw. You'll notice how the creators then factor those hypothetical outcomes into their design decisions. Coding for insight is what we have observed time and again when we manage to create the conditions for young people to develop products that lead makers and users to question, interrupt, and disrupt normative ideologies, forming new ways to understand and make the world.

From Topic to Story

Where we stepped out of our gentrification brainstorm, the team members had shifted from a topic (gentrification) to a specific format (an interactive map), and were starting to dig into content. What information will appear on the map? What larger message will that content deliver? Also, what knowledge sources hold authority? The team pushed beyond an "official" narrative to envision an interactive experience that centers the experiences and expertise of the very people getting displaced in a changing community.

"And the residents of West Oakland would probably definitely have something to say about that. I know that they notice it happening," says Yonas, once again broadening the array of voices factoring in the team's ideation. He relies on his own knowledge of West Oakland residents—his family and neighbors—to make a case for how invested the community will be in the interactive we create. Again, he's showing us how user-driven design can't be reduced to a discrete phase of research but instead threads through the process of formulating a vision for a product worth making.

"How would you go about telling that story and what might be the visually attractive element?" Ike prods, once again seizing an opportunity to get more specific about the user experience the team has in mind. "Would it be a map with layers? Pictures that you could peel back over time? . . . Something along those lines?"

"Gentrification changes neighborhoods," another student states—an attempt to sum up the project's big idea.

"Hone it down a little bit," Ike urges.

"There is a cultural divide between the old and the new," notes Yonas.

"All of these private industries are just coming in. . . . They're sucking away the historical value of our community and what we had," Kendrick asserts.

"How things have changed, and what these changes mean, and perhaps the implications that they have," says Yonas, expanding Kendrick's frame.

Across this exchange, youth and adult participants build on, validate, question, and counter one another's contributions. As educators with decades of experience working in a range of learning environments both inside and outside school classrooms, we know not to take these types of conversations for granted. Young people take risks, show their vulnerabilities, and yet remain open to new perspectives that lead to critical thinking and insights about the world. This kind of talk tends to indicate projects that spark genuine engagement and are heading in generative directions.

And yet it is not lost on us that the young people are, at this point, still to some extent avoiding Ike's question: What will we actually make? What will it look like? What media will it contain? How will users move through the experience? What tools and skills will be necessary to build it? The young people have already accomplished a lot. They've broken down complicated topics into component parts, identified patterns, and come up with a model for how to represent information in a way that achieves a desired outcome—all dimensions of data science literacy and computational thinking, broadly defined.[2] But they have not yet quite arrived at an actionable design. So the work continues.

Data and Design: From Story to Specifics

Ike asks us to jot down a few historical and cultural landmarks that could go on our story map, and we discuss the merits of each one.

"DeFremery Park is definitely a big landmark," Kendrick offers, and Yonas agrees, "especially for the [Black] Panthers." Kendrick reminds us that the Brown Berets, a Chicano organization that started in the 1960s, held a large rally with the Black Panther Party for Self-Defense in 1968. The two groups, alongside others, gathered at DeFremery Park to protest the politicized and dubious incarceration of Huey Newton, the cofounder of the Black Panther Party.[3]

"What about the Black cowboys?"

"How about the jazz clubs on Seventh Street from the forties to the sixties?"

Only through our collective sociopolitical and historical knowledge are we able to make decisions about what to include and exclude.

"So if you haven't done sketching, this would be a good time to move on to sketching!" Teresa calls out from across the room, reminding us of the deliverables at hand. As Yonas attempts to draw out the shape of Oakland, we talk about the various interfaces of the map.

"Is it a map with sounds?" Ike asks.

"Should it be formatted for mobile or should it be a web app?" Yonas wants to know.

"I'm thinking more of a web app in my opinion," Kendrick offers.

"With maybe an option to tag things?" Ike adds.

"Like, pinpoint certain historical events that have happened," Kendrick suggests, and adds that we should include a feature that allows us to zoom in and out of various locations.

At this point in the conversation, we've moved from abstract ideas to specific features, and this is key. Implicit in each design choice will be a set of requirements for data and coding skills that the intergenerational team will rely on to turn these imagined features into reality. Again, this is computation in service of insight, and not just any insight, but a critical understanding that the makers have determined is necessary for their community to meet the challenges ahead, to hold its history in the face of change.

As we get into the details of the interactive, debate erupts over the landing page. Yonas grabs a marker and starts drawing upside-down teardrop icons on the map of Oakland to connote the important historical cultural landmarks we've started to identify.

"Maybe it should take you to a whole different page with text and audio, and just the history of that area, but without making it too dense because people have terrible attention spans," he proposes. Yonas's been working at YR for a while so has learned a thing or two about audiences and how they're likely to respond.

"So what will we focus it on?" Ike wants to know. "Is it the oldest memory of that place and something from now?" Again, he's pushing for the concrete—in this case, maybe a "before" and "after" comparison.

"Yeah, and it should be how things have changed. For example, we used to have barbeques here every Saturday, but then my uncle moved to Antioch and nobody works the grill anymore."

Yonas's example of his uncle is indicative of a rapidly changing Oakland. In 1980, Black people made up almost half of "the town's" population, but by 2015 that number had dropped to just under a quarter.[4] Conversely, in Antioch, a suburb forty miles east of Oakland where housing is a lot cheaper, the Black population in 2015 was more than twelve times what it had been twenty-five years prior.[5] Exclusionary housing practices—"state violence and dispossession, extrajudicial violence, exclusionary zoning, racially restrictive covenants and homeowner association bylaws, racialized public housing policies, urban renewal, racial steering and blockbusting, and municipal fragmentation and white flight"—have most certainly played a role in the Black exit from Oakland.[6]

Cognizant of these forces at play and in an attempt to bring all the group members into the conversation, Cliff asks a student what he would like featured on the map. "I'd like to see a lot of landmarks, a lot about famous people you wouldn't know about," the student responds. He imagines a use case: a tourist coming to West Oakland, coming across a building, and being like, "Oh! What is this building about?"

That remark sparks a new level of discussion: Who is this interactive for? It occurs to the group that there is only so much we can control about who uses what we create or how. We raise the possibility that the map could backfire, essentially "packaging" the community in such a way that makes it even more attractive to outsiders who will contribute to the trend of driving up costs and undermining culture, pushing long-term residents out. We continue to return to this scenario and other cautionary tales as the group goes forward from ideation into the next phase: researching, designing, developing, and distributing a project we come to call *West Side Stories*.

Making It Real: From Design to Build

It's striking to notice how many of the core features that made it to the final version of *West Side Stories* were established in this initial ideation session. The format of a map. The historic locations. The embedding of first-person voices from local, longtime residents. The icons marking key places throughout the neighborhood. That said, the young people and their adult collaborators would continue to work for months to design and code these preliminary ideas into reality.

Building on this first brainstorm, the youth team pitched various detailed concepts for the map, including features that could have been great, but outstripped our capacity and timeline. There was an idea for a "heat map" filter that showed where displacement was most concentrated; a dateline slider across the bottom that would allow a user to move back and forth through the decades, and watch iconic locations appear and disappear from the map; an interactive guide showing how not to be a jerk when you move to a new place; and a tracker that would invite community members to report "sightings" of lesser-known cultural symbols—like statement facial hair or certain kinds of vintage hats—the young people viewed as warning signs that gentrification was coming or proof that it had arrived. Even though these user experiences did not make it to the final build, going through the process of fleshing out each one was highly worthwhile. It enabled the young people to imagine more elaborate future versions of their project beyond its "minimum viable product," and forced the group to get more and more specific about exactly what the interactive would and would not do. Key points across our development cycles reveal how insight continues to accrue at the intersection of critical social analysis, computational thinking, and creative expression.

Why the map: When the team landed on a map as the format for *West Side Stories*, that one decision made it possible for our lead developer, Lo, to establish a code base for the design. They accessed an existing open-source project whose basic flow was similar to what our team had in mind. The project was created by a developer named Young Hahn, who had used a tool called Map-Box to tell an interactive story about Sherlock Holmes. Hahn had published a tutorial in which he shared his starter code and process of combining geolocated data with narrative, thereby helping to inspire and inform our approach. The basic user experience was there. A vertical column ran down the left edge of the screen listing key points to visit, and then a map filled the rest of the display, featuring those locations where they exist in the world. As you scroll down the vertical column, stopping to click on descriptions, the map moves you to the street address where each location appears. While we had to modify Hahn's code, which had deprecated, his skeleton enabled Lo to teach the basics of map creation with the MapBox tool. Working collaboratively with our novice developers, Lo would write lines of code and then leave instructions so the young people could fill in the blanks, and thus in the process learn important computational concepts like coordinates and objects in JavaScript.

The young people wanted their map markers to be customizable—not just the upside-down teardrops that Yonas envisioned in the initial brainstorm, but shapes that contained zoomed-in versions of drawings they'd produce of the locations that the marker pointed to on the map. So Lo adapted the code to make that experience possible, working with the young people to understand how to create that effect. This is just one example of the interweaving of critical social analysis, computation, and creative expression grounded in lived experience that propelled the production process forward through every stage. With each decision, the young people, and their adult collaborators, arrived at new levels of insight into the experience they were creating and the phenomenon of gentrification they aimed to share with their audiences.

Why history: All through that development process, members of the team kept revisiting a set of existential questions for the project. What exactly are we trying to accomplish? What value do we bring? What user takeaway is most important to us?

"What kind of app is it?" Teresa asked at one point. Should it be built as a web-based experience or a mobile app you'd download from an app store? The team considered the pros and cons of each option, returning at one point to the specter of tourists swarming the neighborhood using the slick phone app we'd made to navigate this corner of the city. This scenario sparked knowing laughter, eye rolls, and Yonas's animated playing out of the scene: all these people "with beards and plaid shirts, like, 'Oh my god, this is SOOOO interesting! Look at all of this history!'" This playful discussion led to a deeper exploration of the intended audience for *West Side Stories*. Finally the group got clear that it was for "both sides," meaning the people who were doing the gentrifying and those who were "getting gentrified" because both had something important to learn from the stories we would share. Their vision for the project's intended audience went beyond this one little neighborhood of West Oakland.

"From a journalism standpoint," Yonas said, "gentrification doesn't just happen in Oakland. It happens everywhere. And I feel like this concept is applicable to multiple situations. . . . I mean it could just be about Oakland gentrification, but by looking at it, it gives you more insight on gentrification overall."

To unlock that insight, all through her leadership of the project, Asha reinforced the importance of history, drawing on personal experience. "My grandfather was born in California. I was born in Oakland. Both of my parents were born in Oakland," she said. "And I think the problem with gentrification and cultural appropriation in general is that people erase your history. Knowing the history, and documenting that history, allows people to maintain their ownership and where they see themselves in the city."

With that kind of understanding in place, the youth team knew to approach even a technical decision, like whether we should create a web-based or mobile app, as a judgment call that would have serious cultural implications. They had to think deeply about what they needed to do to make something that honored a history at risk of disappearing. We circled around this commitment not just in one discussion but repeatedly.

"I'm thinking, why is history so important?" Khalil said. "Talking to myself like, 'Self, how is history important?' . . . Because when you look at the past, . . . there are specific events that are preserved because they are important. People think like, 'This is something that other people need to know.'" By producing this interactive, the youth team joined the ranks of those in a position to determine what people need to know. That is an empowered place to be. Because, as Khalil pointed out, "if you don't pass down history and talk about it, it's like it never happened."

Look, feel, and sound: Every detail of the final design of *West Side Stories* was intentional, including the use of light and airy pastel colors—shades of purple, pink, turquoise, seafoam green, and butterscotch gold. The youth team was determined not to default to expected iconography and typography that played into stereotypes of urban design, like graffiti-inspired letters and dark, gritty colors and surfaces. These aesthetic judgments leveraged the young people's deep knowledge of what appealed to them and turned them off, combined with their awareness of trends in digital design—for example, a move toward buttons that looked flat instead of three-dimensional. This sensibility would keep their visuals fresh and current.

For each location featured on the final map, we assigned members of the team to trace photos using a simplified hand-drawn black outline, which accomplished several things. It created a visual consistency across the map, solved digital rights issues we would have run into had we sourced photos for each, and conveyed the human care that each one of the youth team members put into this product that came to mean so much to them.

They had to capture, produce, and organize a great deal of content to appear on the map: longitudinal and latitudinal coordinates, location descriptions, audio and video links, fact-checking verifications, red-green-blue-alpha color codes, and those hand-drawn illustrations. We used a detailed, shared spreadsheet, which each of us would update in real time as we brought in the data. That said, from a user point of view, the finished product, while not entirely devoid of numbers or statistics, dwelled in the land of stories.

Rain, one of the lead youth designers, made the case for creating a highly visual and personal experience to capture what gentrification means for the community where it happens: "If I'm looking at an app or looking at a website, I don't want to read through the numbers. I kind of just want a visual representation so that I can look at it . . .

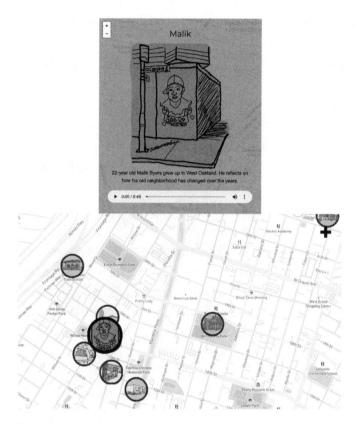

Figure 3.1
Screenshot of YR Media's *West Side Stories*.

because if I wanted to go through the numbers, I would have gone through the pages of data." In the end, *West Side Stories* is a collection of images, voices, and narratives.

We visit Hotel California, a 1920s' building that is now low-income housing, but started as a place that welcomed Black artists and musicians when they were discriminated against elsewhere.

We witness the turf dancers who regularly come onto the BART trains at the West Oakland Station to perform feats of flexibility and grace using the vehicle's seat backs and poles to defy gravity as well as the limits of the human body.

We meet Joyce Elaine Carter, aka Miss Cookie, who has lived in the neighborhood for thirty-seven years and vows she's not going anywhere. "Now all of these white people coming down here buying all the houses and I don't think that's right. . . . I paid $15,000 for my house. And I'm staying right here."

We experience an open house for prospective condo buyers, including one person who says she's looking for a property that she can rent out using Airbnb, and another seeking a neighborhood with "a little bit more diversity and flavor than what we've been able to find on the San Francisco side."

We look at the mural off Tenth Street honoring US Olympic sprinters Tommie Smith and John Carlos, the gold and bronze medalists, respectively, in the two hundred meter who stood at the podium during the 1968 Summer Games, bowed their heads, and raised their black-gloved fists as the US national anthem played during the victory ceremony. This location on the map is unique because it marks something that no longer exists. The West Oakland building onto which the mural had been painted was used as a decontamination station. Once that work was done, the structure was bulldozed, taking the artwork with it.

And finally, there is twenty-two-year-old Malik Byers, who stands on the corner of Fourteenth and Campbell, and grapples with his mixed feelings about the changes playing out everywhere in the neighborhood he calls home:

> When I first moved here, the neighborhood was predominantly Black. Cool little neighborhood, but it was kinda rundown. They're starting to fix it up, for the newcomers, you know. BART is looking good. . . . It's for them. I do like the way Seventh Street is coming about . . . becoming more peaceful. But the only way this is coming about is because all of these white folks is moving in here. At the same time, us Black people, we've got a responsibility. We shouldn't let outsiders come in and take our neighborhood from us. We should have kept what we had nice and protected it, and maybe we would have had a different outcome.

CCE in Unison

Writers work in the medium of words. Illustrators work in line, color, and composition. Audio producers use sound. Web developers use code. Interactive producers like the team behind *West Sides Stories* need to integrate all of these elements into a whole that's sufficiently compelling to entice users to engage—to click, swipe, listen, and watch. Those working in the spirit of CCE need to go one step further, constructing a narrative that brings users along in their social analysis and maybe even inspires action.

Details as seemingly minute as the order in which to arrange the media in the column to the left of the map have major consequences. If we placed Miss Cookie's raw testimonial about her frustration with the white people buying up the homes around her as the first location on the map, might that draw some users in and send others away? Would sandwiching her audio between two pieces that highlight Sixteenth Street Station and the Port of Oakland help users grasp the historical gravitas of her statement? With CCE, creators must be conscious of all three spheres, and how to leverage each of them to develop a product that is cohesive, engaging, and transformative.

Digital Afterlife

After months of work, through cycles of ideation, design, research, content and creative asset production, development, and testing, finally YR Media published *West Side Stories*. It was picked up by various high-profile outlets, including NPR, *Vox*, and the *Atlantic*. It spread via social feeds. Educators working in community programs and classrooms from elementary schools to graduate courses used it to teach new groups of young people about gentrification, urban studies, media representation, youth multiliteracies, and digital storytelling. We performed segments of *West Side Stories* at a live event and created an installation based on the project as part of an exhibit at the Oakland Museum of California. At one point, a lifelong Oaklander and justice advocate who had opened a grocery cooperative on Seventh Street took issue with the way Byers described the market in his audio clip, as if the place were a product of gentrification as opposed to a community resource made by and for devoted long-time residents. He reached out and let us know. So Yonas went out to the market, just blocks from his own home, and interviewed its founder. And we created a new post featuring that interview as part of an expanded version of *West Side Stories* that we called *Oaktown*, mapping gentrification across five neighborhoods in the city.

When we code for insight, we do it for moments like this. Moments when what we make from code, pixels, and people's lives goes out into the world. Once there, it sparks new understandings and conversations that are nuanced, challenging, ongoing, and vital to us all.

4

We Code for Connection and Community

Community Stories

For most of their lives, *West Side Stories* producers Kendrick and Yonas were raised in and by the Oakland community. They have felt the exploitation caused by generations of redlining, structural disinvestments, housing displacement, and now gentrification. They have heard stories of how eminent domain severed their community in half—first by a freeway, then by a subway line, and finally, by the construction of a post office, which took up six city blocks and obliterated over four hundred homes. They saw what happens when schools lack basic resources and have a turnstile rotation of teachers. This is not, however, their single story of West Oakland.[1]

Their identities are also shaped by the rich legacy of jazz and blues on Seventh Street, known as "Harlem of the West" in its midcentury heyday. They have been shaped by the audacity and pride of the Black Panther Party along with its radical demands for Black freedom, fair employment, education, housing, health care, and an end to police brutality. Their communities benefited from the Panthers' creation of the free breakfast program in schools. And by doing the research and interviews on *West Side Stories*, they gained deeper insights about themselves and their history.

For her recording on the map, Ericka Huggins, the former director of the Black Panther Party's Oakland Community School, told them that their neighborhood park "was used for rallies, food giveaways, art displays, music, everything you can imagine."[2]

They strengthened their appreciation for their own families, as Kendrick reflected: "There was a time where there were offers for our house . . . There was a time we had struggled financially. However, with my mom seeking [additional] education, she ended up getting more opportunities for work and is now the breadwinner for our family."[3]

They connected with fellow teens and young adults like Josh Clayton, who struggled to navigate the violence on his block. "My little cousin looks up to me, and that makes me uncomfortable because I don't want to mess up his dreams. But the best thing for him, *and* me, *and* Oakland too, will be to take on that challenge and be a mentor to him. I'm trying to remember that I have a voice and the power to change the future . . . We all make the future."[4]

By collecting voices from the past, connecting them to the present, and sharing them with their communities, the makers of *West Side Stories* worked to shape that future for themselves and their city. As their ideas for the project developed, the youth team members referenced neighborhood murals, back-in-the-day block parties, and corner stores. They traded nuanced observations of the changing landscape. They were not simply completing an assignment for YR Media. They were sharing a sense of where they came from, and what cultural, political, and social antecedents defined them. The project created an opportunity for them to elevate the stories of the individuals, institutions, and cultural landmarks that made them who they are as well as helped to set in motion the forces that impact them today. By curating these stories through an interactive map that cuts across time, they produced a collective narrative of West Oakland forged by struggle, and bonded through resiliency, resourcefulness, hustle, creativity, strength, and wisdom.

After *West Side Stories* went live, educators, activists, and community members well beyond the Bay Area got in touch, eager to extend the project into their own neighborhoods. They shared in the exasperation and anger evident in the voices of *West Side Stories*, and in the inspiration to organize and challenge the unscrupulous political maneuverings that exacerbate displacement in their communities. What began as a brainstorm between two teens who had grown up blocks from each other culminated in a team of thirteen young people and adults creating a dynamic digital experience that resonated with thousands of people across the United States.

Coding for Connection and Community

We introduced *West Side Stories* in the prior chapter as an example of coding for insight. There is a second, equally important context for understanding the project. *West Side Stories* both formed out of and reinforced connections and a sense of community among its creators, and between them and their audiences. When youth producers know their work has the potential to reach a single user, or hundreds, if not thousands, their sense of purpose shifts. They start to see how their media provides a platform and tools to navigate hostile systems, dismantle barriers, and build solidarity. They become agents of change, capable of educating and galvanizing people who were strangers through the products they design. In the process, they change too. They develop a capacity to persist through uncertainty and struggle because they aren't alone in trying.

The sense of connection and community we seek extends beyond the team of creators to include the audiences that take up our stories and make them their own. Educators have long understood the power of connecting learners to authentic audiences. What's new in the current moment is that so many of the young people we work with are already reaching audiences through their own social media platforms, without our involvement or even awareness. Our youth collaborators are used to receiving near-instant feedback on the images they share, memes they repost, videos they like, GIFs they send, and thoughts they tweet.[5] And yet despite their constant digital connection with others, we're also seeing evidence that young people are feeling increasingly isolated and lonely—more so now as a result of the global pandemic that forced so many of them to shelter at home.[6] This paradox of connection and isolation raises the stakes of our work to code for community. We push ourselves to leverage the communication tools that young people use everyday while working to erode the obstacles that keep them from one another and their audiences. The possibility of creating genuine connection is what drives the work—the chance for a sense of belonging.

Our process begins with young people identifying deep dilemmas or burning questions that matter to them. It makes a real difference when a project as arduous as researching, designing, developing, and distributing an interactive story originates in the creators' authentic interest. When young people take on truly daunting problems, they have no choice but to lean on one another to produce the best possible product—not for an individual grade or a teacher's approval, but because they are mutually invested in the potential impact of what they create. To glimpse what that investment in connection and community looks like, we turn now to *Your Queer Rights*.

Your Queer Rights

"If you are in a place where maybe you are the only queer student in your class, [you may wonder] 'Why are people being mean to me?' If the only thing that we're doing is showing you that there are other people who look like you, identify as you, who have fought for your rights, and reminding you, you do have rights, that's one [person] who we changed here."

This is how Asha, at the time a twenty-five-year old Black, queer YR Media graduate who went on to cofound and lead the organization's interactive department, framed the significance of the *Your Queer Rights* app. By speaking in the voice of the imagined user, our team leader helped us shape our agenda for the project's aesthetics, functionality, and purpose.

Rob, sixteen years old, white, trans, and one of the original cocreators of the app, concurred. "I think it's really important to have the specific legal code to give people concrete evidence and have that empowerment," he said, and then, voicing the message of the app, he added, "Look, you may feel small now, but there have been people in the past who fought for you and there are people *now* who are fighting for you. And this app is proof that people still care about you."

For Rob, the project was personal.

> I was a young, angry child. I was filled with a vengeance that I no longer have. So I think for me, at the time when we first came up with the idea, I was really kind of PO'ed at the world because I had just started getting into the [LBGTQ+] community and I was really new to that . . . When I was younger, I was like, "Screw those people who are causing fear. That's not cool." And it isn't. I think in my relationship with the app, it went from being like [that, to], "I wanna do something."

Rob traces his emotional journey from anger and isolation, to wanting and needing to be a part of a larger community of shared collective struggle, resilience, and agency.

Eventually, nine young people and four adults would work on the *Your Queer Rights* prototype. They used a tool that our MIT partners had created called App Inventor. It's a blocks-based coding platform that allows novice programmers to develop Android apps. Although the design and features of the project shifted over time, the core remained. Together with Rob, Kenji, fifteen years old, Asian and white, designed *Your Queer Rights* app to create "a sense of community" for LBGTQ+ teens and young adults.

From Personal Struggle to Project Ideation

YR Media's interactive projects usually take off when young people find a personal connection to a social issue and discover how coding can help them do something about it. Rob, half the youth team, and nearly all the adult staffers that led the development on the project were a part of the LBGTQ+ community. The stories they'd reported in the past included the use of LBGTQ+ terminology; identity, love, and coming out for nonbinary youths; and the importance of trans representation in the media. "Who are better prepared than the oppressed to understand the terrible significance of an oppressive society?" wrote critical theorist and practitioner Paolo Freire. "Who suffers the effects of oppression more than the oppressed? Who can better understand the necessity of liberation?"[7] While Rob and the other members of the *Your Queer Rights* team may not have used the term *oppressed* to describe themselves in 2017, they most certainly identified with the experiences of LBGTQ+ peers who regularly face stigmatization, criminalization, institutional barriers, discriminatory public policies, derogatory political rhetoric, microaggressions and physical assaults, and prejudicial school and health care systems that favor heterosexual, cisgender communities.

Freire argued that those who shoulder the heaviest burdens are the ones who will lead themselves and others to freedom. But how? For Freire, the key is praxis, the constant negotiation between critical reflection and action on the very structures that bind them. Education can make it possible for people to experience their conditions "not as a closed world from which there is no exit, but as a limiting situation which they can transform," wrote Freire.[8] This view is evident among the Black church members who nurtured activist communities in the fight against Jim Crow segregation, Mexican and Filipino farmworkers in California who demanded fair wages and humane treatment in the Delano grape strikes, and LBGTQ+ activists who rose up during the Stonewall rebellion. Through collective action, these communities found hope, camaraderie, and healing.

YR Media has long worked to support the well-being and tell the stories of LBGTQ+ communities. So when Rob and Kenji pitched this interactive, the questions were less about whether to green-light the project, but instead how to get started.

Beyond Alerts

What should the app do? Why and how would a young person use it? How does it benefit them? What protections do we need to implement to ensure they are safe? Our team cycled through these questions again and again throughout the process of making *Your Queer Rights*. That's the case for all of our projects, but especially one like this, where we were considering asking users to share personal information that if we were not careful, could put them in harm's way. Also, our plan was for the app to feature laws designed to protect LGBTQ+ teens from discrimination and violence. If users relied on our tool for a situation as serious as that, we knew there was no margin for error.

One of the original features of *Your Queer Rights* was an alert button. The idea was that a user could preprogram the contact information for select friends and family members into the app so that if they needed help, with the push of a button they could send a prewritten text message sharing their location. Despite the potential power of this feature, the team grappled with its limitations. They created a survey polling LGBTQ+ young people and adults, and discussed among themselves the pros and cons of the alert feature—in this way sharpening their product plan, and grounding their choices in the actual needs and practices of the community they were a part of as well as sought to engage. "Who

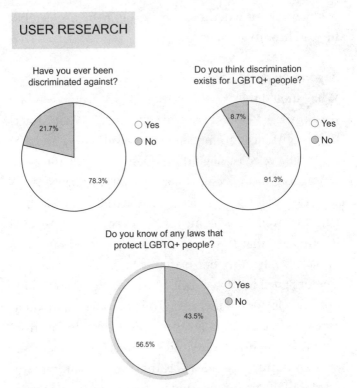

Figure 4.1
Slide from a "Demo Day" presentation where young people shared early research informing the design of *Your Queer Rights*.

do you contact in a time of emergency?" Rob asked the group at one point. Pretty much everyone said their moms or a close trusted adult. "If I wanna call my mom, I'm gonna use the phone," Rob said, remembering the team's thought process. "I'm not gonna go through a separate app. That's just not gonna happen. So that was scratched because . . . it wasn't gonna be used."

In place of the alert button, the team turned to a report feature. It would allow users to document and share a description of an incident where they felt they'd been discriminated against because of their LBGTQ+ identity. The team wanted young queer people facing cruelty or bias to have a resource that drew a clear line between bullies being mean and abusers breaking the law.

The team designed features that allowed users to capture and time stamp photos, recordings, and text-based descriptions as evidence. "The best way to keep someone accountable and respect your rights is to document everything," the team wrote in a wireframe where the report button appeared. "If you choose to report to someone, to the principal, authorities, or social media, facts and evidence are your friend. We'll help guide you through this process."

Tapping resources and experts from Lambda Legal, the American Civil Liberties Union Transgender Law Center, and the Gay-Straight Alliance Network, the team drafted a series of questions to help users determine whether an incident they'd experienced was discriminatory.[9] We considered rewriting laws in youth-friendly language, but realized that was too risky. "When it comes to saying, 'These are your rights and the law,' you don't really wanna mess that up," Asha explained, realizing how easy it would be to accidentally introduce inaccuracy. There was also something empowering that Rob saw in featuring technical terminology, word for word. "Soon as somebody tries to screw with you,

you can pull it out and be like, 'Well according to 10–09 Section V, you can't do this. It's against the law and I could sue you.'"

One final dimension of the report feature the team included in the prototype was the ability to view previous reports so that users could see they were not alone in their struggles. This feature threaded an awareness of connection and community into the design, bringing users together in a feeling of shared experience. For Rob, the ultimate goal of the app was for queer young people to know how they could take action. "You can say, 'Oh, my school is maybe being terrible to me about which bathroom I can use at school.' And then all you have to do is look at the app and be like, 'Oh, actually, this is against the law. They can't do this.' And you've got resources right there that it'll link you to, that'll explain exactly why and where in the law it says that."

As we mapped key points in the making of *Your Queer Rights*, we were reminded once again of our framework for learning as meaningful participation in communities of practice through projects that center the experiences of those with the most at stake in the issues they explore and therefore the most to gain from the products they design. Freire's notion of praxis was a guide throughout, as young people cycled through periods of action and reflection, just as they moved through frames of computation, critical analysis, and expression to translate ideation into code. They collected data, created wireframes, tested features, enacted use cases, and then together made sense of what they were learning, revamping their designs accordingly. For those on the team who were part of LGBTQ+ communities, standard questions took a first-person form. Instead of asking, "Why and how would a young person use this app?" or "How would it benefit them?" they asked, "How can it help *me* and *my friends*? How can *I* make this app better for *myself and my community*?" When we code for community, creators dream beyond the confines of the present reality and toward a more connected world where belonging is possible, enabled by products of their imagination, one feature at a time.

There was an additional feature of the *Your Queer Rights* that wasn't about rights at all. After researching legal codes for weeks and weeks, and designing the app's report feature, Rob raised a concern. Would it be enough for the app to identify laws designed to protect people from discrimination? Asha sensed a need for some other element. She suggested featuring a different LBGTQ+ icon with inspirational quotes each time you opened the app. Even within LGBTQ+ communities, Rob felt "there's a lot of erasure of trans men and nonbinary folk," so this new idea would provide a way for the team to expand the range of leaders recognized for their roles in the community. Another member of the team, a queer Black teen, took on the task of researching over forty leaders, including many young, contemporary activists. She used a spreadsheet to collect the data and then had a producer in the newsroom fact-check every line. The carefully curated images, biographies, and quotes that appeared as part of the icon feature acknowledged the collective historical traumas that LGBTQ+ communities have endured while highlighting narratives of resilience and joy, bringing about that sense of belonging we seek by coding for community.

"Work as an Ensemble": Coding in Community

At YR Media, job responsibilities—graphic artist, programmer, user experience expert, and researcher—often blur, and this was certainly the case with *Your Queer Rights*. After the ideation and wireframing process, Asha assigned two high school teens who were more seasoned programmers to take over the development using App Inventor. One of those programmers spoke candidly, saying the code she inherited "looked really wonky, and some of the things weren't working as smoothly." So she and her partner cleaned it up. Along the way, Damian and Desean, two of YR Media's in-house illustrators, were tapped to translate bare-bones wireframes into full-blown designs and visual assets. Other young people and adult staff members around the YR Media building tested, brainstormed, and answered survey questions to optimize the user experience.

"Everyone's in charge of the product," Asha reflected. "It needs to be something that somebody wants to do . . . For all of them, for every project . . . No matter what your role is, you can make suggestions to the experience . . . We weren't going to say that just because you don't remember the JavaScript function, that you couldn't say, 'This didn't work well'"—and why.

This inclusiveness can be challenging with so many points of view in the mix, but within the YR Media world, diversity of experience is an asset. The *Your Queer Rights* team was made up of students who attended large, urban public schools, racially diverse suburban schools, and a small, high-tuition private school. We had students who were multiracial, Black, white, and Asian. Students struggling to graduate with minimum GPA requirements worked in tandem with those applying to Ivy League universities. It's rare for young people to find themselves in such diverse collaborative teams, and more unusual still for those teams to be designing technology for widespread use. And yet this range of perspectives among the designers is needed for apps like *Your Queer Rights* to connect with the broadest possible audience.

"I think just the way that we work here at YR Media is we collaborate and we work as an ensemble," is how Damian put it, reflecting on their role as a designer of the project.

> And I think that can be one of our strengths. It also makes it hard to get work done when there's different visions for a project and people are trying to take it in different ways, but I don't think that happened very much in this example. There might have been a little bit of, "Oh, I think it should look like this." "No, I think it should look like this." In this case, it really

worked to have a lot of different voices because . . .
there was a lot of opportunity for people to give their
feedback . . . I feel like I added something, but I also
don't feel like I could have done that myself. It was
really good to be a part of a team.

We'll give Rob the last word on *Your Queer Rights* as a
product of coding for connection and community.
Due to school responsibilities, after working through
the initial design phases of the project, he stepped back
for three months. "I was totally exhausted . . . just being
like, 'I'm so done with coding!'" But when he came back
and saw the spruced-up App Inventor code, updated look
and feel, and the new icons section, he was delighted
when he saw evidence that some of his original development work had made it to the final prototype. "That's
my code!" he exclaimed. Even one of the lead creators
didn't take for granted that his contributions, including
his novice code, belonged in the finished work.

Mood Ring

Starting with the Self: Leveraging Community Cultural Wealth

Two teens, Terrell and Nala, came to the interactive
department at YR Media in summer 2015 from vastly
different public high school experiences—one with over
two thousand students, and the other with fewer than
two hundred. Both are young Black people who were

passionate about teen mental health. For three months prior to joining the interactive team, Terrell and Nala worked in YR Media's health department, where they participated in peer-to-peer workshops on a range of topics including dating violence, wellness, sustaining positivity, bringing forth awareness of your feelings, and physical health. Once they came to interactive, Asha started the session with a broad assignment for the new group: create an app related to adolescent health. Initially, the group kicked around the usual stories about nutrition and exercise. But when the members really thought about their friends and classmates, Terrell said their focus shifted:

> There are a lot of suicide rates. There's a lot of angry teens, and they don't know what to do with their emotions. Some people turn to drugs. Some people do violent acts, which land them in jail. We were just thinking, what's a simple way to talk to teens or see how they're feeling without them doing things that will cause them harm or others harm.

What Terrell and Nala noticed among their peers is a well-documented phenomenon.[10] Young people in communities like East and West Oakland can experience trauma and post-traumatic stress syndrome at higher rates than soldiers, according to the US Centers for Disease Control and Prevention.[11] And yet unlike soldiers, who eventually come home from deployments, young people cannot necessarily extricate themselves from the sites and sources of their trauma.

The challenges can be heightened as a result of disinvestment in public transit, inadequate housing, police violence, lack of job opportunities that provide livable wages, property crime, and the criminalization of substance use in urban communities. Numerous research studies have demonstrated the range of stressors that can affect youth mental health, particularly Black, Indigenous, and Latinx teenagers who contend with material insecurity and social structures upholding white supremacy.[12] They are more likely than their white counterparts to live in communities with high rates of violence.[13]

Asha's prompt to the youth team opened an opportunity for the young people to see these realities with open eyes, grapple with them, and then take action. What if you had a way to track your moods through an app on your mobile device, using the same emoji you use to text your friends? And what if that app uncovered patterns in your emotions over time and sent a report to you, at your discretion, and your most trusted friends when you need support? This was the impetus for the creation of the *Mood Ring* app.

Challenging Intuitions: Complementing Lived Experiences with User Research

One way to understand the context that grounded the work on *Mood Ring* is Tara Yosso's notion of community cultural wealth, or "the array of cultural knowledge, skills, abilities and contacts possessed by socially marginalized groups that often go unrecognized and unacknowledged."[14] The group started by turning inward. What do I do when I'm upset or stressed out? What do I do when I am struggling with all kinds of feelings? Nala described her circle of friends' reliance on one another to get through turbulent times. "We [use] emoji all the time, telling each other how we feel. We would text each other, 'What you doing?' and put a sad face. 'Oh, what's wrong?' Instead of writing it out . . . It's easier than typing."

Starting at the project's inception, the team members knew that they wanted their app to offer emoji as a way for users to express themselves. And they understood that when they experienced dark times, friends were critical sources of support. "After we came up with our original idea, we started to do surveys and . . . user research to see what people would want on that app," Terrell said. "And then, we did market research to see other apps that were similar, . . . and [see] what theirs did and what theirs didn't do, so we could make ours better."

Their survey results from seventy-six youth at YR Media were striking. Almost half of their respondents said they would not talk to a therapist or call a hotline. When asked, "Who do you go to when you're having a problem," they overwhelmingly pointed to their friends (76.5 percent), followed by their parents (28.4 percent) and siblings (19.8 percent). When asked to pick five emotions to describe what a teenager feels in a given week, "stress" was

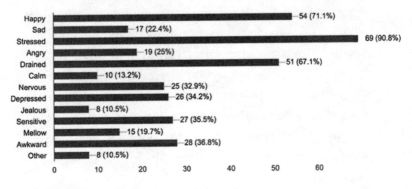

Figure 4.2
Youth survey results of emotions that teens feel in a given week.

nearly unanimous at 90.8 percent, followed by "happy,"
"drained," "awkward," "sensitive," "depressed," and "ner-
vous." The survey findings suggested that designing an
app that centered peers as resources and addressed the
high levels of stress young people reported made a lot
of sense.

The idea began to form that the app would prompt
young people to record their emotions so they could
build self-awareness, notice patterns, and share "reports"
with trusted others. At this point, the team revisited
Nala's insight about emoji. "We were trying to make an
easier way so teenagers can express their emotions," said
Terrell. "Teenagers spend a lot of time on their
phone nowadays, so we just [came] up with a simpler
way for them to express their emotions without having
anger issues or just going off on people, and can write
how they're feeling."

That said, they hadn't yet refined the user experience. They needed once again to tap community knowledge. "We just thought that people would just want to press [an] emoji and that would be it," said Nala. "[The app] would track it, and you would know what it means."

Luckily, the team members had included questions about emoji on their survey as well, and they were surprised by the results. When asked, "How do you [prefer to] describe your emotions—with emoji, words, or both?" respondents preferred a combination of words and emoji (42.9 percent) over emoji alone (2.5 percent). So the team members added a field to their design where users could write reflections and provide context for their emoji choices.

Coding for connection and community means keeping an open and inquisitive mind, seeking and applying data to produce technology that is responsive to user habits. The youth team needed to balance personal experiences with research to confirm or challenge its hypotheses. Its orientation framed the community as an asset-rich resource, not a broken system that technology could fix.

The user research informed another aspect of the app too. "We added daily affirmations," Nala said, "daily quotes to send you to uprise your feelings." Nala came up with the idea using herself as a proxy for the target user. She had several affirmation apps on her own phone and appreciated how they uplifted her mood each day, so she urged the team to include this feature in the design. Survey respondents indicated this addition would be an enhancement. These are the benefits of being a designer who is also a member of the community that the team is creating for; there's a lot less guesswork as to what users want when the app developer is one of them.

Community Support for Mental Health

The data that the *Mood Ring* developers factored into their design decisions came from a range of sources, including systematic research with their peers via surveys, reflection on their own habits and inclinations, and tapping experts for feedback and advice. This work aligns with Yosso's notion of navigational capital, meaning the capacity to maneuver through social institutions including those that do not center your communities' well-being.[15] Mental health institutions in particular tend to fall far short when it comes to providing culturally sustaining care. In the design of its own case management services, YR Media set out to counter those institutional patterns with staff members who integrated healing-centered and justice-oriented culturally relevant practice into their approach. So for the *Mood Ring* team, YR Media's case management department was an important resource within the young people's community to inform the app's design. The team interviewed one of the resident therapists, Stefan, for feedback on its plans.

He offered useful critique. Stefan noticed that when the interactive team members spoke with him about the project, they would casually refer to "negative" emotions. He urged them to reconsider that frame. Even potentially painful emotions, he said, like sadness or anger, can be reasonable and necessary responses to a person's situation. Classifying them as negative can pathologize rather than support young people who are struggling. Conversely, he pointed out that so-called positive emotions, like happiness, when experienced in excess and without interruption, can be a cause for concern. When he sees a rich range of emotions over time in his clients, that's generally an indication that they're doing okay.

These considerations had significant implications for *Mood Ring*'s design. The team members rethought their approach to the "Emotion Tracker" feature so that it would graph users' feelings over a two-week period—the interval that Stefan said clinicians use to notice if a persistent pattern is setting in—and they added a prompt encouraging users to pay attention to variation in their moods. In this way, the app aligned with professional best practices for building skills for self-awareness and resilience.

Stefan also noted that a marker of adolescent development is the capacity to feel more than one emotion at the same time. Again, this psychological insight had implications for the team members' computational effort. They'd need to rewrite the code that initially enabled users to pick just one emoji so as to make it possible for them to pick as many as felt true from a set of twelve options.

Nala was especially taken by the value of the Emotion Tracker in the way that it would allow young people to "reflect on themselves . . . [and notice] 'I was sad, mostly the whole week. I need to not do this . . . and not be with that person.'" Awareness empowers young people to connect their moods to specific behaviors, relationships, or situations in their lives, and thus "be more conscious [of] their well-being . . . and [make] the right choices," including recognizing when they may need the help of others. Terrell explained how the app promoted outreach for support:

> When you start up the app, it's going to actually [ask you to] put [in] personal contacts, as in relatives or friends. So just in case you're having a problem or you're feeling really down, it'll alert them. . . . "I think you should check on this person because they're not feeling good this week," or they put too many sad or mad, depressed emoji, or they're feeling like they're going to hurt themselves. It'll just alert them and be like, "Hey, how are you doing? Are you okay?"

When faced with institutional barriers and biases, young people rely on their social network of friends, family members, and community resources to help them move through bureaucratic systems that are often not created for them.[16] *Mood Ring* continues traditions found in Black social networks, National Association of Colored Women's Clubs, and immigrant communities of lending material, physical, and emotional support to one another.[17] The app's creators harnessed mobile technology as a tool to find and share resources from within their networks and themselves.

In the final phase of the project, the *Mood Ring* team tested its design once again—this time not through a

Figure 4.3
The interactive youth team documenting insights from its user testing of the *Mood Ring* app.

survey checking hypotheticals but instead via sessions where peers could actually try out the app and offer feedback.

Mood Ring's makers relied on candid feedback from their intended users before finalizing their design. The goal was not only to identify bugs or glitches before publishing the product but more fundamentally to ensure that what they created would be of authentic use for the community they were a part of and aimed to serve.

Data Privacy and Digital Afterlife

A final consideration in *Mood Ring*'s design pushed us to revisit the past in our programming for the future. While the team worked hard on the feature that enabled users to update trusted friends and family members with emotion reports, there were no automatic alerts on *Mood Ring*. Users needed total control over their personal information and decisions about disclosure. And emotion data were only stored on an individual's device, not the cloud. The app's creators knew about the long and troubled history of researchers, government officials, health care workers, and police mining personal data from BIPOC and other hypersurveilled groups without their consent.[18] The team's approach to data privacy and security drew on that critical awareness. The question of how to store user data might seem like a technical matter. But to answer that question, the team members needed to understand their community's rights and past harms as well as appreciate the preciousness of what they were asking users to express about themselves. They grasped what their responsibilities were to ensure that the app handled that information with appropriate care. In this sense, even the design of something as computational as a data storage structure needs to be interrogated in relation to critical ethics and creative expression.

We are coming full circle with the theme of coding for connection and community here. While the goal for *Mood Ring*'s creators was to better the lives of other teens, they in turn gained greater insight into themselves. "I noticed that when I'm emotional or upset. . . . I go straight to my phone," said Rain, a twenty-year-old member of the interactive team who worked on *Mood Ring*. "I think we use our phones as a distraction.

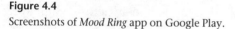

Figure 4.4
Screenshots of *Mood Ring* app on Google Play.

Making a mobile app that uses a distraction and turns it into something positive is really powerful. It promotes a lot of healthy processes that can really help a young person engage into how they are feeling rather than putting up a wall." Rain and her peers seized an opportunity to program their mobile devices as tools for personal and community self-knowledge, care, and empowerment.

Little Rock Nine Live (LR9LIVE)

Three years after the US Supreme Court ruled that segregation was unconstitutional, nine Black students enrolled in the all-white Central High School in Little Rock, Arkansas. In September 1957, they arrived for their first day of class, only to face a threatening crowd and national guard soldiers deployed to block their entrance.

Sixty years later, a group of current Central High students reached out to YR Media to see if our newsroom could help them tell the story of the Little Rock Nine. The students were part of the Little Rock Central High Memory Project, an oral history and civil rights initiative geared toward intergenerational learning.[19] Today's Central High students wanted to make events that took place in their town more than a half century ago vitally relevant to communities across the nation now.

Working with the young people at Central High and youth colleagues in Oakland, two YR Media producers, Teresa and Nancy, came up with an intriguing way to bring that oral history to life. They issued this provocation: If Twitter were around in 1957, how would the Little Rock Nine story unfold? Also, how do the themes and conditions of the original Little Rock Nine connect to racial inequality and school resegregation today?

We called the project *Little Rock Nine Live* and gave it the hashtag *#LR9LIVE*.[20] On the morning of September 25, 2017, we began tweeting archival pictures, videos, and quotes from the perspective of news reporters at the scene at Central High. We posted artist renderings of the Little Rock Nine along with quotes from the first days of desegregating their new high school. The interactive team developed a microsite to house the content so that communities could continue to engage with it after the commemorative day. The project combined computational thinking, analysis of inequalities past and present, and dynamic creative assets, from freehand digital illustrations to carefully composed narratives. In this sense, it fully manifested the CCE model.

It seemed fitting to use the twenty-first-century tool of Twitter to immerse today's students in a stirring confrontation with segregation's enduring legacy. Packaging the experience in contemporary digital technology shrank the distance between "them" and "us," "before"

Figure 4.5
Screen capture of *LR9Live* Twitter story.

and "after." *LR9LIVE* fostered an honest reckoning with the past so that students across the United States could understand how we've arrived at the racial dynamics we're experiencing today, and what more we can do, have to do, to combat inequality and bend history toward justice.

As with all of YR Media's interactive products, audiences became participants in the narrative as it unfolded. They read, liked, and responded to tweets, in some cases adding their own commentary and questions.

The tweet above highlights the use of archival photos combined with contemporary Twitter discourse to educate present-day audiences about the heinous actions of segregationists in 1957. Notice the string of question marks and emphasis on adults versus teens to convey the author's appalled reaction to the picture. The use of hashtags connected the topic to other conversations on Twitter, sparking engagement through retweets, quote tweets, and likes. Through quote tweets in particular, users added layers to the story and shared their reflections on their own timelines, broadening participation in the discussion by bringing in new followers.

@mistydawnu and @_elisaramos added their emotional reactions to the archival photo and tweet that YR Media had shared. @girlact75 and @Michelle_IC compared the effigy in the photo to a mock lynching of students who simply wanted to attend an equal school. @bellinissima questioned the education of the adults who were

Figure 4.6
Screen capture of *LR9Live* Twitter story.

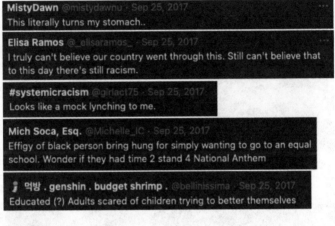

MistyDawn @mistydawnu · Sep 25, 2017   ...
This literally turns my stomach..

Elisa Ramos @_elisaramos_ · Sep 25, 2017   ...
I truly can't believe our country went through this. Still can't believe that
to this day there's still racism.

#systemicracism @girlact75 · Sep 25, 2017
Looks like a mock lynching to me.

Mich Soca, Esq. @Michelle_IC · Sep 25, 2017
Effigy of black person bring hung for simply wanting to go to an equal
school. Wonder if they had time 2 stand 4 National Anthem

🎵 먹방 . genshin . budget shrimp . @bellinissima · Sep 25, 2017
Educated (?) Adults scared of children trying to better themselves

Figure 4.7
A selection of quote tweets following one of YR Media's *#LR9LIVE*
posts.

attacking students for pursuing a basic human right.
@Michell_IC posed a tongue-in-cheek question that
connected the events in 1957 to 2017 debates about
athletes kneeling during the national anthem to protest
police brutality and racial inequity.

The producers of *LR9LIVE* used social media and web
design to tell a multidimensional story that went far
beyond the kind of static, single-authored account
you might find in a textbook. Audiences could interact with and imagine themselves in the story, refram-
ing the typical relationship between reader and text. In
addition to the social media content, *LR9LIVE* included
an audio essay that aired on NPR from Central High
junior Zia Tollette, who questioned the effectiveness of

past desegregation efforts based on observations of her school today:

> Central is desegregated. But like many schools across the nation, it's not exactly integrated. These divisions are clear-cut: Black students eat in the cafeteria, white students eat on the patio. Central has AP, or advanced placement classes, but those classes tend to be mostly white. As a biracial Black and white female, it can feel like I exist between two worlds. Even though people of different races go to the same schools in 2017, we are not necessarily living in the same version of America. . . .

Rebecca Martin
@rebm

Students: what needs to happen for integration to be real in schools today? What's the 1st policy move you want to see? @youthradio #LR9Live

10:18 AM · Sep 25, 2017 · Twitter Web Client

2 Retweets **2** Likes

Marybeth Gasman @marybethgasman · Sep 25, 2017
Replying to @rebm and @youthradio
Families have to care about all children and not just their own. When we care about other people's children, we all benefit. #LRLive9
♡ 1   ⟲ 1   ♡ 2

Maya Mj James @MissMayaJames · Sep 25, 2017
Amen
⟲   ♡ 1

Figure 4.8
Screen capture of *LR9Live* Twitter story.

> So every year, when my classmates and I revisit the story
> of the Little Rock Nine, I don't just celebrate the freedoms
> we've won. I think about the battles still to come.[21]

Tollette's account of the de facto segregated spaces within Central High reflected the long-term psychological, cultural, and political impacts of institutionalized racist policies. Her story provided a through line connecting the historic events of the Little Rock Nine to her experience as a multiracial student at the same school sixty years later. In a tweet responding to Tollette's essay, YR Media deepened that connection: "Students: what needs to happen for integration to be real in schools today? What's the first policy move you want to see?"

"These Are Like My Ancestors"

Twenty-one-year-old Desean was the graphic artist for *LR9LIVE*. Teresa asked him to create nine portraits of the teenaged civil rights leaders that would establish the look and feel of the whole project. When asked why he chose to create original color illustrations rather than simply reproduce the archival black-and-white photographs supplied by the Memory Project, Desean referred back to the project premise. "I would guess having it black and white would kind of make it seem like a long time ago," Desean said. "You're trying to make it more . . . alive, like today." The goal, he noted, was for the audience to be "feeling like you're living through this or you're experiencing it."

Taking the point of view of anticipated audiences, as Desean did here, was a go-to technique on the interactive team. Producers imagined how future users might respond to the tiniest subtleties in their interfaces, such as fonts, copy, colors, and graphics. In order to achieve the purpose of *LR9LIVE*, Desean knew connecting to history in a visceral way was key. Black-and-white photos wouldn't go far enough.

So he worked out a plan that leveraged his computational and artistic skills to solve the problem of how to render the nine Black students who made history that day. He was stymied by the limitations of the archival pictures. "The young pictures," he said, "there wasn't . . . a lot for me to really work with." The newspaper photographs from 1957 didn't provide important details that Desean was looking for to create truly vibrant images for a social media feed today. Age was not the only factor that degraded the quality of the available images. Photographic equipment and techniques had been calibrated based on white skin, too often underlighting Black and Brown subjects, and yielding images that flattened their full, distinctive humanity.[22] It was yet another institutionalized form of racism that shaped civil rights history, evident in visual details available in the artifacts that remained.

Desean searched for more recent images of each of the Little Rock Nine students, now adults. He used a combination of their pictures from their teens to their forties to represent who they were. Attentive to diversity in skin tone, highlights, shadows, and other distinguishing

Figure 4.9
Screen capture of *LR9Live* Twitter story.

features that marked each student's likeness, Desean came up with a technique for creating accurate and indelible portraits, moving between the photographs he had found online and the layers of line and color he produced using digital tools.

Desean's artistic process leveraged his algorithmic problem-solving skills. He framed the scope of the problem, identified relevant details, broke the issue into component parts, established a logical sequence of steps, and finally applied them to arrive at a solution: the dynamic set of color portraits that came to define *LR9LIVE*.[23] More fundamentally, the project also tapped something profound for Desean as a young Black artist whose own life had been shaped by this event he worked so hard to capture.

> It's connected to my history. These are like my ancestors.
> It was pretty cool. Because this is *Brown v. Board of
> Education* so I felt like I was kind of reliving that too,
> just because as I'm drawing them, I'm going back into
> history and restudying everything they did. . . . With
> this project, it really made me tap in, and it really made
> me get to know each person as I was drawing them.

Teresa and Nancy did not make it a requirement for Desean to study the history of the Little Rock Nine and the *Brown v. Board of Education* Supreme Court case. He did that on his own accord, gathering the research he felt he needed to do justice to the narrative. "I wanted them to look good," Desean said. "I don't know if any of them has passed, but if they look at it, I want them to be like, 'That looks like me, that looks good.' Or just people who actually know what they look like, I want them to be able to just look at them and say, 'Oh my gosh, that looks exactly like them.'" He imagined the audience reaction he was after, and then called on the critical, computational, and creative resources within himself and his community to turn that hoped-for vision into reality.

Desean's process has a lot in common with the other producers whose coding for connection and community we have explored in this chapter. When young people immerse themselves in complex projects with consequences that matter in their communities, this set of conditions intensifies their engagement and promotes the excellence of their products. We witnessed these outcomes when Kendrick, Yonas, and their *West*

Side Stories collaborators fanned out across their changing neighborhood to capture and map its vital stories before it was too late. We felt the urgency and passion in Rob's voice when he pushed for the inclusion of laws that would empower LGBTQ+ communities in the face of discrimination. We recognized Desean's drive when he labored to get the nine portraits just right. The profound insights and intuitions that these creators possessed came from collective experiences with struggle, resilience, and problem-solving. They drew on intergenerational ideologies, discourse practices, and epistemologies. They took in data that challenged their assumptions and then reframed projects in light of new information. In so doing, they developed products that both emerged from and created conditions for culturally sustaining, justice-driven communities of practice.[24]

5
We Code for Accountability

Double Charged: A Case of Impact

In 2013, YR Media launched an ambitious juvenile justice investigation. Through our day-to-day work with system-engaged young people and a program we ran with incarcerated teens, we had noticed something deeply troubling. Again and again, our students and colleagues, or their family members, would pick up additional charges not because of a new alleged offense but rather because they had failed to pay court-assigned fees attached to their original detention. For every night a young person spent in juvenile hall or every day that they wore an ankle monitor, they would get a bill for the associated costs. When those fees were transferred to adult caregivers, a parent or guardian could have their wages garnished if they missed payments. Here is how one story from our series began:

> Ricky Brum stood in an alleyway behind a furniture store in Manteca, California, and to be honest, it was a little awkward. He didn't really want to be there. Last

February, Brum set some cardboard boxes on fire just a few feet away.

"Just that right there," he said, pointing to a black spot on the pavement. "Just a little burn mark on the floor."

One match did the trick, said Brum. "Like, I just sat there and was like 'Bam!'"

That "bam" changed Ricky Brum's life. He was 15 when he set the fire. It was his first time getting in trouble with the law. He was lucky: his charges were reduced to a misdemeanor. Brum went on probation and to juvenile hall.

Brum and his mom Leanne thought the worst was behind them. But then, while meeting with their public defender, they found out about restitution.

"We thought it was a joke," said Leanne Brum.

Sitting at his kitchen table, Ricky Brum flipped through the restitution claim. Even though the fire department report said there was no damage to anything in the furniture store, the owner claimed his entire inventory of nearly 1400 items was smoke damaged.

The bill came out to $221,000.[1]

Brum's story was just one case in our investigation, which we called *Double Charged*. Another young person we wrote about in the series had been an intern at YR Media—an active member of our music and health departments. At seventeen, he'd been picked up on a charge that he and his mother maintained was a case of mistaken identity. Nevertheless, he served 56 days in juvenile hall, and 152 days at a boot camp in Mendocino, California. In June 2012, he was shot and killed in Vallejo, California. Even two years after losing her son to gun violence, his mother continued to be billed.

"The bills are an additional stress to already a very painful situation that I will be dealing with for the rest of my life," she said.

Double Charged included audio and written features, infographics, and videos for national and local radio as well as print outlets, including NPR's *Marketplace*, KALW radio station, and the *Atlantic*. A key piece in the reporting was an interactive experience we produced for our website titled *Double Charged: Behind the Numbers*.

"In the juvenile justice system, young people charged with a crime can be subject to jail time, probation, and fines and fees," we wrote to set up the interactive. "Youth Radio's Innovation Lab invites you to explore these stories to see how court-related debt can add up." From there, users could choose among three composite characters, Jeremy, Jason, and Gina, whose stories were based on YR Media's reporting carried out over more than a year. "The names are made up, but the details are real," we noted, "drawn from interviews and county averages."

After picking a character to follow, the user clicks through various key points in that young person's story, from their original alleged offense through the accumulation of fees that came with it. The $300 public defender fee. The $540 supervision fee. The $200 investigation fee, which is assigned even if the young person is found innocent. The restitution order originally set for more than $200,000. Against a backdrop of black-and-white photos showing scenes of juvenile detention without revealing individuals' identities, the interactive moves through the phases of investigation, sentencing, restitution, and outcome for all three characters. With every step, a calculator in the lower left corner of the screen adds up the accrued charges. The final screen displays the total amount charged, links to the full *Double Charged* series, and invites users to "tell us your story."

Double Charged was honored as a Media for a Just Society Award finalist. The series aired on American Public

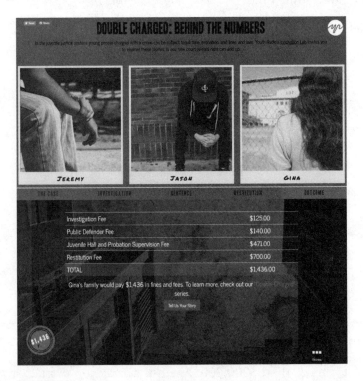

Figure 5.1
Screen capture of *Double Charged* interactive calculating the total fines and fees.

Media radio and local stations. Stories were published by the *Atlantic* and *Buzzfeed*. These outcomes alone would have made a big difference for the creators, the young people and families featured, the organization's sustainability, and the audiences that learned about deep problems in the juvenile justice system through our reporting.

And then this happened.

"Last week, the Alameda County Board of Supervisors passed a moratorium on the assessment and collection of juvenile fees," YR Media reported in a 2016 post. The moratorium ruled that "no youth or his/her family shall be assessed juvenile fees by the County," and "no youth or his/her family who has been previously assessed juvenile fees shall be required to pay outstanding amounts."[2]

Our very own county would stop charging young people and their families the court-ordered fees that caused such financial hardship disproportionately affecting those already contending with poverty and related challenges.

YR Media was notified about this news by someone who'd played an important role in helping us understand the undue and unequal burden created by juvenile fines and fees in the first place: Kate Weisburd. At the time, she was a supervising attorney at the University of California at Berkeley's Youth Defender Clinic at the East Bay Community Law Center. Weisburd credited YR Media's investigation for our role in this policy outcome.

> *Double Charged* shined a spotlight on a critical problem in the juvenile justice system that until now has

received no attention. The Youth Radio series provided
a vivid picture of how court fees detrimentally impact
the families of court involved youth and push them
further into poverty. The stories helped spark a
conversation between advocates and policy makers
about reforming the imposition of court fees.[3]

We also heard from the mother who had been receiving
bills in the mail for years after her son had been killed.
Though she welcomed the news that Alameda County
had put a stop to juvenile fines and fees, the new policy
didn't apply to her case. Her son's charges came from a
different county. "It was only because of the story you
did (and that I had a reference to use)," she wrote in an
email, that she had the courage to call up that county
to discuss options. "Thankfully after reviewing my case"
she told us, "I heard back from them that I now have a
0.00 balance. I can't express how thankful I am not to
have to get those reminders in the mail." It didn't stop
there. In the years after our story and interactive were
published, and Alameda County changed its position
on juvenile fines and fees, other counties followed suit.
In 2017, five other Northern California counties passed
similar legislation. "On January 1, 2018, California
became the first state to abolish all administrative fees in
juvenile delinquency cases."[4]

Double Charged hit a high mark for YR Media as a
case of coding for accountability. It traced a direct line
from our young people's lived experiences, through the
organization's reporting across a broad range of formats
and outlets, supported by juvenile justice reformers and

mentorship that our staff provided to affected young people, all the way to a life-altering and long-overdue shift in state policy. Events like these point to what's possible when we partner with young people, and harness the power of computation, creative expression, and a critique of injustice to tell necessary stories in the most dynamic ways we can devise. That said, if we organized our entire production company around this level of impact as the only valid measure of success, we would serve far fewer young people, and we would miss far too many opportunities to hold power accountable in less dramatic but still significant ways. Accountability, after all, takes diverse forms.

Coding for Accountability in Action

When we design digital products that hold powerful individuals and institutions responsible for operating in ethical and equitable ways, we code for accountability. The work might start with a brainstorm where we analyze how best to represent the perspectives of teens in foster care navigating the child welfare system. Coding for accountability might take the form of a mobile app that educates the public about the laws that protect queer young people from harassment; an interactive that points users to movies on Netflix with Black, Brown, and LGBTQ+ leads; or a web-based calculator that tracks the fines a young person who's been arrested is obligated pay on top of their sentence.

In each one of these cases, our team created interactive products that carry out one or more of the following: highlight the voices and perspective of groups that contend with interlocking, unjust systems; bring attention, awareness, and visibility to social issues that impact these groups; and/or provide tools that they can use to navigate and challenge systems and advocate for transformative change.

Holding people and institutions accountable for their actions can span a spectrum of tactics. Organizers for social justice carry out legal fights in courtrooms, political education in communities, public service announcement campaigns, investigations into corrupt or unfair practices, banner drops, marches, public demonstrations, sit-ins, and so on. Coding can be a tool that supports each of these tactics and more. Speaking truth to power through code requires creativity, resourcefulness, a theory of change, and a plan of action. Young people can use computation—together with design, data, and investigation—to develop multimedia products that interrogate normative practices, expose wrongdoing, shift ideologies, and empower people to act.

Over the past ten years, we have developed more than twenty interactive projects that have elevated the voices and perspectives of teens and young adults navigating the multilayered effects of white supremacy, patriarchy, and runaway capitalism. Through these products, we have called out the child welfare system, schools, mental health providers, and juvenile (in)justice systems that fail the very young people they purportedly serve. We have tackled issues related to the #OscarsSoWhite, #Never-Again, and #MeToo movements to bring accountability to the entertainment industry, gun policy, and sexual misconduct, respectively. We have reported on multinational technology companies that use AI and personal data to bolster profits without sufficiently accounting for ethics or the potential for harm.

Coding for accountability is especially salient given the young people who come to YR Media. Many do not have the privilege to choose how they would like others to identify them. Their mere presence can assign them a label of "at risk"—problems to be solved rather than creators of solutions. We have watched and joined them as they have created products that directly interrogate flawed labels, systems, and institutions. Interactive products that lack any grounding in sociopolitical awareness and interconnectedness with others fall short of their full potential as drivers of change. That said, creating interactive digital products is hard work. It almost always involves periods of confusion and the dreaded experience of backtracking to fix errors with elusive solutions. For many young people, the motivation to keep going comes from a strong desire to bring about social impact—the possibility of igniting systemic change for themselves and others.

And sometimes, that motivation starts with an everyday observation, like when members of our youth team started chatting one afternoon about the arbitrariness of school dress codes. That conversation set them on a path to pull together a national data set, and produce an interactive digital project that calls on users to think critically about the ways in which school regulations can smuggle in gender, racial and class-based bias.

What If You Ruled the School Dress Code?

Micah was a junior at a local Catholic high school. One day she arrived at YR Media and told us a story about something aggravating that had just happened to her. She and her mom were getting ready to leave the house, Micah for school and her mom for work. Heading out the door, they laughed when they realized they were wearing almost exactly the same outfit. The two shared a fashion sense and so the situation was not uncommon for them. But this time, when Micah got to school, she was immediately "dress coded" by an administrator, who determined that her shirt was cut too low. This was not the first nor the last time that staff members at her school would make this kind of proclamation and punish a student for it. The day after being dress coded, students were compelled to wear "liturgy attire"—a buttoned-up shirt with a prim white collar—to learn a lesson.

Micah thought maybe her school was especially strict because of its ties to the church and that her peers at public schools wouldn't be dealing with the same unevenly enforced restrictions. Two girls on our interactive team made it clear that was not the case. Shaundra, a senior in a large, public high school in Oakland, and Mia, a junior in a small, public charter school in Oakland, both related to Micah's sentiments. "It's very subjective," Shaundra said. "Some teachers will call you out on something you wear, but other teachers wouldn't." They were a racially diverse group. Micah is white, Shaundra Black, and Mia Latinx. Taken together, members of our interactive team at the time represented six different high schools, and across their experiences, we began to notice similar themes of arbitrary, discretionary, and inconsistent school dress code policies and practices.

This was just the beginning of our months-long investigation into dress codes across the United States. The more research we did, the madder—and more motivated—the young people got. Their individual experiences evolved into deepening, shared understandings of institutional practices propped up by sexism, racism, and the upholding of middle-class norms.

The project appealed so much to the team in part because of its potential scale and relatability. Dress codes affect "everyone at a young age," in Arianna's words, and they "teach kids a messed up image . . . that what they're doing is wrong." Arianna, an Asian American sophomore at the time, attended a different public high school than Micah, Shaundra, and Mia.

"Typically, there's more scrutiny on girls' clothes," said Julia, who is Black and nonbinary, and had recently finished college. "Femininity is sold in stores to girls of a certain age as certain clothing. And so a lot of stores don't sell school-appropriate clothing." Micah built on Julia's point: "What you're told to wear by all of society and what you see is very different from what you're told is appropriate at school. So it's really confusing. You don't know what to think or how to act because you're getting two completely different messages." The team knew gender would be a theme in its interactive. Schools tended to police the cut of a shirt or top, length of dresses and skirts, and width of a strap. Codes that applied to, say, T-shirts mainly focused on the *content* of the attire: images and texts alluding to sex, violence, drugs, and alcohol.

Micah: So girls' dress codes are usually more directed at covering up your body.

Shaundra: Yeah.

Micah: Which delivers . . . a really different message than what guys get. So when you're told, like, your shirt is cut too low, it's like what does that mean?

Alex (interviewer): What *does* that mean?

Micah: Well, it means that you're not allowed to show that part of your body, which sexualizes girls to [start with] at a young age. . . . So basically telling you that this part of you isn't allowed to be shown somewhere because . . . it's distracting to someone else. That's the underlying message.

Julia: Yeah, girls' shoulders are just so polarizing [sarcastically].

Alex: Oh, like you're not allowed to show shoulders?

Micah: Yeah, at my school you can't show shoulders or collarbones.

Shaundra: Like you can't have spaghetti straps or not even like one-inch-width straps. Your shoulder has to be completely covered.

Alex: Collarbone is named?

Shaundra: Yeah.

Micah: Yeah.

Alex: Wow.

Micah: The clavicle. So it's also completely arbitrary because it's like, this is the line and no one knows why that line is there. Especially for me, at least as a high schooler, it's just a completely arbitrary line drawn to control something that I don't have any control over. And then I'm in school learning about arbitrary laws and government.

Something important surfaces out of this conversation that might not be obvious at first. Whenever we're making an interactive, there's a key step where we move from a qualitative experience to a case we can make with data. At some point, we have to be able to identify relevant information, and count, plot, or organize it in such a way that tells our story. For *West Side Stories*, that meant identifying a finite set of locations, and finding their longitudes and latitudes so they would appear correctly on the map. For *Double Charged*, that meant collecting records showing the fees assigned to specific mechanisms of juvenile supervision and detention, and feeding those into our calculator.

For *What If You Ruled the School Dress Code*, Alex pushed to understand details on how dress codes played out inside the schools that our young people attended. In their responses, Micah, Shaundra, and Julia identified specific body parts—shoulders, collarbones, and clavicles—policed by their schools' policies. This level of precision is necessary to tell an interactive story. When we move from a personal narrative to a digital experience, we need to know what counts in one category (for example, permissible based on a given school's dress code policy) versus another category (for instance, a policy violation). Even before the team members settled on what data we'd collect, organize, and ultimately display using computation and design, conversations like these were crucial. They advanced ideation from intuitions and impressions toward specific, observable data that could make a powerful point.

Ideation and Research

When creating an interactive product whose central purpose is to hold a group, institution, or system in power accountable for its actions, data science and journalistic skills are vital. With the dress code project, we had several ideas that didn't make it out of our ideation phase. One of our team's initial ideas was to curate outfits from popular fast-fashion retailers like H&M and

Urban Outfitters, and ask users to guess whether the looks would violate the rules at various schools. The interactive would provide the answer based on policies we'd collected in a national database. And the playful outcome would be that none of those outfits would meet dress code standards in most schools. Another idea was to reach out to young people who had tagged their posts #DressCoded or #IAmNotADistraction on Twitter and Instagram to report problematic run-ins with school administrators over alleged dress code violations. When we noticed the lack of racial, gender, and body-type diversity across those feeds, we knew we'd need to broaden our sourcing beyond those hashtags. We ruled out some ideas on principled grounds like the previous one. In other cases, we nixed compelling concepts because we knew that even with the relative flexibility and freedom we enjoyed as an out-of-school media organization compared to, say, a CS classroom, we didn't have the necessary financial or technical capacity to pull them off. Accountability operates in this sense as well: we hold ourselves to a standard with our young people to scope out realistic projects we can finish. Despite our best efforts, as we will see in this chapter, we do not always succeed.

Over the course of several weeks of research and ideation, we learned how gender, the sexualization of female bodies, body type, race, class, and culture influence school dress codes in the United States.[5] In a sample of California schools, we discovered that 70.8 percent of the prohibited dress and grooming practices targeted girls along with Black and Brown boys.[6] In a study of 481 public high school dress code policies in the United States, 77 percent described the policing of certain body parts, specifically, in order from the most common to the least: midsection (71 percent), cleavage (22 percent), back (15 percent), breast (14 percent), and buttocks (11 percent).[7] It is clear who these policies are intended to target.[8] The underlying message to girls is: you are responsible for how others see you and how they respond to your self-presentation. For boys, the message is: you are not capable of controlling your actions.

We discovered that self-objectification can cause young women to underperform on math tests and be tied to restrained eating and low self-esteem.[9] Over the past decade, there have been several high-profile examples of Black children being told that wearing their hair in natural locs or braids was not fit for school.[10] Too often, these racialized codes were disguised under seemingly innocuous language like "neat," "clean," "well-groomed," or hair that is not "distracting" to others.

Grounded in this research, we engaged in several wireframe feedback cycles. Individuals, pairs, and small groups would draw what they imagined our interactive could look like. Everyone would present their wireframe, answer questions, and receive feedback from peers. Figure 5.2 is a collective design that includes ideas from the entire team.

As you can see on the left side of the whiteboard, the "goals and messages" that the team had in mind spanned a range of angles: how dress codes differently affect young people depending on gender and ethnicity; what an inclusive dress code would look like across a fluid gender spectrum; how codes determine who gets to wear what; how people's personal accounts of dress code enforcement relate to official policies; and how people's reflections on past experiences with dress codes change over time.

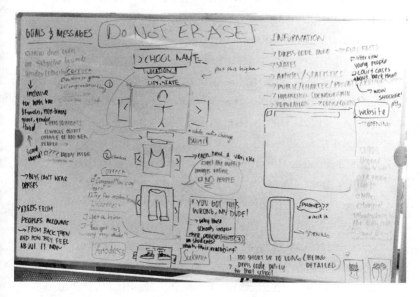

Figure 5.2
Image of a collective wireframe brainstorm for the *Dress Code* story.

The middle portion of the board (below "do not erase"), took its cues from the 1990s' movie *Clueless*. The film's iconic main character, Cher, was so rich that she had a program on her desktop computer prepopulated with her seemingly endless wardrobe options. Each morning before school, she would click through different combinations of tops and bottoms, and preview what they'd look like before making her choice. Our youth team members envisioned functionality like Cher's as a core feature of their interactive: a kind of clothing carousel where the user could swipe through garment options. In our case, instead of picking a fabulous look for school, the interactive would either accept or reject an outfit based on dress codes from various regions across the United States, with results such as "Congrats! You can learn" or "You got this wrong my dude!"

The young people's use of popular culture for inspiration reveals the difference it makes when the people designing an interactive are also its target audience. They have a sense of the cultural reference points—in this case, 1990s' nostalgia—that will resonate with their peers. Once users are hooked by a shared sensibility or experience of fandom, they're primed to take in a deeper accountability message. Additional team notes in this section imagined an option where the interactive would not only publish excerpts from actual policies but also the rationale that schools used to justify them, which we could investigate through our reporting. This aspect of the concept reflects the team's interest in offering context to enhance users' understanding of the motivations and intentions behind the policies.

Finding the Story in Data

Our ambitions for the dress code project were national, so we used audience data to identify locations throughout the United States that would allow us to look for regional differences in dress code policies: Oakland, New York City, Atlanta, Denver, Anchorage, Phoenix, Seattle, Portland, and Jacksonville. From there, we came up with a list of forty-two schools from these cities and their surrounding communities. We compiled and synthesized as much information as we could find on a spreadsheet, as seen in figure 5.3 below.

City	state	type of school	school size	Tuition	School Demographics Data	Demographics Link
Oakland	California	public	1,900-2,100 (2016-17)	None	Black: 28.8%, White: 24.2%, Asian: 20.2%, Multi-racial: 5.8%, Hispanic: 16.7%, Filipino: 1.8%, Native-American/Pacific Islander: 0.5%, None reported: 2.6%	http://www.ed-data.org/school/Alameda/Oakland-Unified/Oakland-Technical-High
	California	private		$42,900		
New York City	New York	charter	400	None	American Indian/Alaskan Native 0.3%Asian1%Black34%Hawaiian Native/Pacific Islander 0%Hispanic64%White0.5%	https://www.usnews.com/education/best-high-schools/new-york/districts/new-york-city-public-schools/university-prep-charter-high-school-138164/student-body
New York City	New York	religious	217	$3,750		
New York City	New York	public	544	None		
New York City	New York	private	1,001	$47,965	White 55.1%; Asian 15%; Multiracial 13.8%; Hispanic 8%; African American 7.8%; Native American 0.3%; Pacific Islander 0%	https://www.niche.com/k12/trinity-school-new-york-ny/students/
Atlanta	Georgia	charter	638	None		https://www.greatschools.org/georgia/atlanta/6635-KIPP-Atlanta-Collegiate/
Atlanta	Georgia	religious	1,080			
Atlanta	Georgia	public	819	None	97% Black	https://gaawards.gosa.ga.gov/analytics/saw.dll?PortalPages

Figure 5.3
Screen capture of the spreadsheet for our forty-two original schools and their demographic information.

In order to arrive at a manageable list of dress code policies to examine in-depth, we worked on narrowing our scope. "People think that different clothing is more appropriate or less appropriate, depending on age," Julia pointed out, "so we wanted the same range of high schoolers, mostly." We also wanted to convey the wide variety of schools across the country, so school size and student body demographics would factor into our sampling, and we opted to include private, public, charter, and religious schools. Our final eight schools covered a broad range in terms of socioeconomic diversity as well. One of our schools had a free/reduced lunch rate of 100 percent, and another had 0 percent. Our final list included three public high schools, one public arts magnet, two charter schools, one independent school, and one Jesuit high school.

As we dove into analyzing the schools' dress code policies, we came across some notable contradictions, inconsistencies, and the aforementioned subjective language.

Shaundra: Oh, Booker T. Washington [high school] also. This is pretty funny to me. They say you can't wear plain white T-shirts. It has it under gang-related or gang-affiliated stuff.

Cliff: Oh, white tees?

Shaundra: Yeah. And it's really funny because some of the pictures of people who actually go to schools with uniforms have white T-shirts.

Depending on the school type, region, culture of the community, and other factors, dress codes varied tremendously, and as Shaundra observed, what stood out as exemplary in one case could be forbidden in another.

Micah, too, was struck by the huge variation we found and its implications: "Where you go can determine what you wear to school, and eventually, who you are." The messages that young people draw from the school regulation of style can seriously shape their senses of identity, self-confidence, agency, and place in society. The codes send powerful messages to teens about who they are and who they should strive to be. "School is where students first form perceptions of the world around them," Hanna wrote in the essay we commissioned to run alongside the interactive. Dress codes reflect points of view that young people carry into adulthood, she wrote, and "ironically, while dress codes might be designed to reduce sexualization at school, the effect for those whose bodies are policed is often the opposite. Suddenly they're being viewed and shamed for how they look."[11]

User Experience That Strengthens the Message

For the interactive's visuals, we decided to take pictures of YR Media students. "Without any preparation, we asked them, 'Can we take a picture of you for our project so we see what [you] actually wear to school?'" Micah remembered.

Seventeen students agreed. We uploaded those images and analyzed them against the eight schools' dress code policies we'd collected from our national scan. It was tricky work, trying to determine which outfits would or would not be deemed acceptable or off-limits in each of the schools. We didn't always agree, and had to keep reviewing the policies and making the case to each other in order to determine once and for all which category each look belonged to, and on what basis. Terms like "offensive," "revealing," and "inappropriate," which appeared in policies, were especially problematic in this sense because their meanings were so subjective.

The difficulty we faced with our inter-rater reliability was, of course, an important finding in itself. We knew from our research that when school policies are discretionary and open to judgment, they are more prone to being discriminatory than those where the standards are clear-cut. "They're very open to interpretation," Julia observed of the policies in our sample, "which, you know, is probably bad for students because if things are open to interpretation, then they can be interpreted wrong." We struggled, for example, with the image of Julia we included in the data set, where they wore a dress and sharp earrings. "Would a ban on an outfit that 'causes distractions or inhibits the learning process,'" one of the phrases we found in our policy database, "make that one off-limits— using the code to enforce gender norms?" Hanna asked. The team created a detailed spreadsheet lining up each featured outfit with relevant excerpts from each school's dress code policy that could conceivably apply.

"A really common one was you can't wear something that is gang related, like certain colors, and you can't have inappropriate images on your shirt, like violent images," Arianna noted. "But is a cartoon of a butterfly melting violent?" she wanted to know, referring to an actual image on someone's shirt in our sample. As Hanna wrote in her essay for the project, "Essentially, if you want to dress like a popular rapper, you are labeled a 'thug' or 'gang member.' These rules put people in boxes and criminalize some of the culture trends associated with people of color."[12]

Rather than eliminate the youth outfits that led to inconsistent results, we made sure to use them since they helped tell our investigation's story. We wanted users to have to grapple with the same challenges that administrators contend with, not always transparently or especially thoughtfully, when they determine what is and is not acceptable at school. This design decision on our part is an example of the data science literacy that students develop through projects like these. They learned that sometimes preparing raw data to make it usable means leaving it messy, especially if that is the story we want to tell.

Once we had the data prepped, and the design mapped out in such a way that would display well on desktops and mobile devices, the youth team worked with Radamés, YR Media's lead developer, to program the project using HTML, CSS, and JavaScript. To build the carousel of youth outfits, our team leveraged GitHub, learning the standards of using and adapting open-source code in the process. The decision to update code that already exists and is licensed in a way that allows future developers to modify it has something in common with a prior decision choice we have already discussed: the use of the movie *Clueless* as inspiration for the interactive's user experience. In both cases, young people glean creative resources and raw materials from the expressive work that other creators have done before them, whether in the context of making compelling media narratives or producing computational features. There is a deeper lesson here about what it takes to produce digital media. It is not a solo process of pulling genius ideas from within. Rather, it's about developing the ability to see what's out there with relevance to the present undertaking, and know how to ethically and skillfully adapt it to the present work. In other words, it is about remixing. This capacity is yet another through line connecting the computational, expressive, and ethics-driven dimensions of YR Media's model for teaching young people to code.

Unlike a typical high school CS course where often the requirements of an AP test and fixed curriculum guides can determine how learning unfolds as well as what students produce, we tend to adjust our curriculum in real time around the products we develop for each session. This customized pedagogical approach places significant demands on our instructors, who are also codesigners and developers with young people in creating projects with no predetermined "right way" to make them work. This dynamic of youth-adult collaboration requires flexibility and a willingness to be vulnerable. Sometimes the technical challenges of a given project can at least temporarily stump even the most experienced programmer. Moreover, our youth teams are strikingly diverse in many ways, including participants' computational know-how, so instructors need to design learning experiences with a range of entry points. Students with more and less expertise can meaningfully contribute through modeling, joint problem-solving, individual / pair / small group work, involvement in pitches and wireframes, and frequent feedback loops to fine-tune both the products we're making and the learning process we develop as we go.

Holding People, Institutions, and Systems Accountable

After months of work, we were ready to publish the final design. When you click on the post *What If You Ruled the School Dress Code*, you are presented with a question: "Do you think the student should get dress coded?" You see a series of three young people, standing in their school outfits. The one in the center is clear, the two on either side are displayed in semiopacity, with little arrows on either side. These are all intuitive design markers that "tell" the user how to interact with the images without having to spell out instructions in words. For each outfit that you move into the center position, you have the option to click "Yes" or "No." Once you've made your choice, you get your results: "You're wrong according to . . ." with a list of schools whose policies contradict your answer, and "You're right according to . . ." followed by the schools with which your assessment is aligned. You have the option to click into each school's actual policy, where you will find the relevant lines or paragraphs highlighted in yellow that we used to determine whether the outfit in question is "in" or "out." (See figure 5.4.)

Part of coding for accountability is planning for a reaction on the part of your users. We anticipated a range of emotions: surprise, confusion, curiosity, satisfaction, incredulousness, and even anger, as users confronted some of the same questions that motivated our interest in the project to begin with. We set out to create an experience that would be more engaging than simply sitting back and reading an article about dress codes. We wanted users to have to make their own choices and see how they held up. This technique of utilizing prediction and anticipation has a long history in literacy research, and has even grown to other disciplines such as mathematics and social science to be powerful in supporting comprehension as well as engagement.[13] This level of participation is what makes interactives stand out, and

Do you think the student should get dress coded?

You're right according to: **You're wrong according to:**

 Booker T. Washington High School
High School
Public
Southeast (Atlanta)
see dress code

Duval Charter School at Baymeadows
K-12
Charter
Southeast (Jacksonville)
see dress code

Seattle Preparatory School
High School
Religious
Northwest (Seattle)
see dress code

Oakland Technical H.S
High School
Public
West Coast (Bay Area)
see dress code

Trinity
K-12
Private
East Coast (New York)
see dress code

Riverdale High School
High School
Public
Northwest (Portland)
see dress code

Frontier Charter School
K-12
Charter
Alaska
see dress code

Denver School of the Arts
6-12
Public Art School (audition required)
Denver CO
see dress code

Figure 5.4
Screen capture of *What If You Ruled the School Dress Code?* interactive.

especially well suited to prompt insight, connection, and action. By using the affordances of interactivity to put users in the position of school administrators, we urged them to grapple with the subjectivity and biases of dress codes, interrogate how policies are applied, and possibly uncover biases of their own.

Creating experiences that force users to reckon with social dynamics that pass as normal, reasonable, or inevitable, but that reinforce inequalities in overlooked ways, is an important move to make across a spectrum of efforts to build a more just world. This accountability work is not the same as, for example, staging a walkout, launching a petition campaign, or lobbying lawmakers on Capitol Hill. The theory of change driving projects from YR Media's interactive department draws on the team's base in a newsroom committed to a particular approach to journalism—one that serves communities that routinely engage with political and social institutions that too often fail those marginalized from power. Digital interactives like *What If You Ruled the School Dress Code?* invite communities to discover information, make meaning from those insights, and apply them to beliefs and behaviors in their lives going forward. The accountability we seek builds on the power of new conversations, grounded in the lived experiences, creative efforts, and computational experiments of young people with so much to teach and learn alongside the rest of us.

Billionaires

There is one more project we want to share to close out this chapter on coding for accountability. We'll say from the outset that it's one we were never able to publish. It didn't get past the prototype phase. Given that, you might reasonably wonder why it belongs in a section of the book centered on bringing about change in the world. What change is possible if a project fails to launch, especially for a media company?

Before we get to that important question, let's look at the project. On Monday, April 15, 2019, phones around the world lit up with notifications, images, and videos of the missile-like spire and roof of Notre Dame Cathedral in Paris engulfed in billowing white smoke and flames. Most of our young people had scarcely traveled outside the Bay Area or California, let alone the United States. They reacted much like you might expect when they heard a faraway old building caught fire and no one died. It didn't register too much in their minds. What did strike them were the reactions of people around the world in the days that followed.

"Wow, $600 million came in really, really fast to repair [this] really old building. . . . I was on Twitter and people were like, 'So we have money for this, but every other natural disaster doesn't get half this much funding,'" Julia remarked. In fact, within twenty-four hours after news broke about the fire, almost $1 billion had been pledged by a collection of French billionaires and multinational corporations along with tens of thousands of individual donors.[14]

The Notre Dame fire coincided with the beginning of a new session at YR Media. The team was weighing potential stories to develop into interactives. The young people could not let go of the juxtaposition of fundraising for Notre Dame versus recent natural disasters around the world. The team brought up the devastating impact in 2017 of Hurricane Maria, which took the lives of over three thousand Puerto Ricans, and led to island-wide power outages, famine, and inadequate medical care for months on end. The young people saw a painfully slow US response to Puerto Rico and a trickle of fundraising. Donations from US multinational corporations were generally in the hundreds of thousands with about two dozen pledging $1 to $5 million.[15] This, compared to the tens and hundreds of millions pledged for Notre Dame. The team members' research also led to a realization that charitable donations often came from millions of regular people's generosity rather than a handful of billionaires. They wanted to create an interactive to spotlight the disparities they had uncovered.

We went through the usual rounds of brainstorms, research, sketches, individual and group pitching, feedback, wireframes, coding, and more discussions. The team members researched which billionaires donated to various natural disasters and tried to calculate how much more they could have helped. They learned about the Giving Pledge, where the world's richest individuals can promise to give back the majority of their wealth.[16] And they discovered that the world's wealthiest person, Amazon CEO Jeff Bezos, hadn't signed it. They read about Amazon workers relying on government assistance for their basic food needs, and that Bezos's donations were overshadowed by those of other billionaires, especially when you consider his astronomical net worth.[17] They decided to use the case of Bezos to tell a story of massive wealth inequality, and its implications when bad things happen and people need help.

As we have seen throughout the book, when making an interactive, at some point the story has to be grounded in data. The fact that Bezos's wealth is best captured through a metric of net worth created a significant challenge for this accountability project. The idea was to create an arresting visual that revealed how much Bezos would have to donate to a social cause, as a percentage of his net worth, to match a donation of, say, $20 from an Amazon warehouse worker. In 2019, "his net worth fluctuates between $150 to $161.79 billion," Julia had cited. But the team members couldn't immediately figure out how to come up with the net worth of an average Amazon warehouse worker. "We can find out the salaries of these people, but net worths are more evasive in terms of data collection. Not that many people know their net worth," Julia pointed out. They tried using wage data, calculating the average annual salary of an Amazon warehouse worker on that basis. When they realized Bezos only took home a base salary of around $80,000 per year, though, they had to come up with a different approach. So they used Bureau of Labor Statistics data to estimate a worker's net worth, which involved factoring in details like age, gender, race, geographic location, education, and so on, to come up with the point of comparison with Bezos. They drew up various user experiences for the project, including a comic book–style story line (see figure 5.5) to walk through the plot points in a

Figure 5.5
Wireframe of the billionaires project.

narrative where an Amazon warehouse worker decides to donate to a disaster and Bezos does the same, but with wildly different impacts on their individual bottom lines.

The team came up with the idea to embed an interactive calculator within the comic. It would match every donation from a worker to what Bezos would have to give, based on their respective net worth. This was a story worth telling.

Yet how to visualize the scale of discrepancy? The team members decided to use a dollar sign icon that they designed to represent the two donations, from the worker and Bezos. But each time they tried to code the interactive in such a way to display small $ icons (how much each would give) inside a larger $ icon (how much their total net worth is), a funny thing happened. The web page crashed. Again and again. Ironically, the very thing that motivated the making of this interactive—the alarming size of the disparity—was our biggest obstacle in producing it. We literally didn't have enough real estate on the screen of a smartphone to fit the outrageously large gap between the two worlds we sought to capture: that of everyday US workers and their boss.

In the end, there's no other way to put it: we ran out of time. And truth be told, the team burned out. As educators, we know that sometimes you have to read the room and realize it's time to call it. The session was ending, and when those who were continuing with the interactive department after a break returned, they were eager to tackle a new project. So we left this one as a prototype, knowing the lesson of what kept us from finishing it was, on some level, the story we were trying to get at in the interactive itself. The scale of inequality was so unfathomably massive, we never managed to wrap our heads or computational know-how all the way around it.

And yet there are deeper lessons here. Even though this interactive did not lead to publication, the team gained powerful insights into global inequality, computational thinking, and creative storytelling techniques. The young people spent months learning about disasters across the world, and the donations or lack thereof that follow; billionaires' net worths; wealth disparities based on race, class, gender, age, and educational attainment; data categorization; big data visualization; and the effective uses of infographics and other formats for visualization. The significance of these lessons comes across when we take a look at what members of this youth team did next. Julia led production on a trenchant, data-rich interactive project about age of consent laws and what they tell us about where legal protections fall short in the context of sexual misconduct. Arianna, another member of the billionaires team, played a key role in our investigation of bias in machine learning algorithms. Even the department's adult staff, experienced designers, researchers, programmers, and educators, the two of us included, learned important lessons from this project as well about how to scope projects so that next time, we could hold ourselves accountable to bringing them all the way through to publication.

Sometimes the impact of digital projects is clear and undeniable, as was the case with *Double Charged*, which won journalism awards and was part of a groundswell of collective activity that led to enduring real-world policy change. Sometimes the impact is evident in the conversations sparked by products like *Dress Code*, which enabled users to imagine themselves in the position of others, and grapple with issues and understandings that have far-reaching implications for education and beyond. And sometimes, the impact resides in the process, in learning the hard way. Even when projects never make it beyond the whiteboards, code bases, screens, and imaginations of the creators, they can promote accountability through the lessons their makers learn by researching and utilizing computational tools to challenge the people as well as institutions that reproduce injustice and inequality.

6

We Code for Creative Expression

In 2018, YR Media launched a podcast called *Adult ISH*. The show's conceit was to follow two BIPOC creatives in their early twenties, Merk and Nyge, as they navigated the uncertain passage from teen life into adulthood. The format of the show mixed expert and celebrity interviews with narrative features where Merk and Nyge shared their personal stories on a range of topics. Friendship, money, mental health, identity, family, politics, sex, and intimate relationships—each of these core life experiences takes on new meanings when we leave adolescence behind. Against the backdrop of the social, economic, and environmental precarities of today, it's become even more challenging to navigate this transition. What definitive experiences even mark off adulthood from the stage that came before? How do you know when you've "arrived"? As you can imagine, Merk and Nyge had a lot of rich material to explore.

In season three of the podcast, they took up a topic that may not be quite as obvious a factor in young adulthood compared to the other timeless themes that Merk

and Nyge had investigated to date. The focus of this episode would be technology—specifically, AI. And they
enlisted help from YR Media's interactive department to
do it.

The YR Media interactive team had made a commitment—and received funding from the National Science Foundation—to spend three years investigating AI
through a lens of ethics and equity. By this point the two
of us, Cliff and Lissa, had been working in and around
media education long enough to have experienced the
impact of earlier waves of digital media innovation. Over
time, YR Media had reinvented its curriculum to reflect
the massive transformation brought on by widespread
public access to the web, and later, social media. Young
people's stories no longer aired via one-way, onetime
broadcasts. They circulated online. Rather than sit back
and listen, audiences searched for, linked to, commented
on, remixed, and in other ways reoriented the producer's
original creation. From the earliest stages of framing a
story, we started to plan not only for its release but also
for what we called its "digital afterlife," a postpublication
period of engagement with the content that could pose
new opportunities and challenges for authors as well as
the impact of their productions.

So when we began to notice more and more evidence
of AI as a driving force in our relationships with technology, media, ourselves, and one another, there was
something familiar in the realization: we had arrived at

yet another pivotal moment that called for a significant expansion of our approach. We knew it was time once again to partner with our youth colleagues to understand how this emerging technology worked, what harms it could exacerbate, and what good it could do. So we launched an initiative, Outsmarting AI. We collaborated with partners at MIT and teams across the organization to learn and tell stories with and about AI, including through the *Adult ISH* podcast.

Most episodes of YR Media's podcast have "ISH" in the title, such as "Working through My ISH," "Me, Myself, and ISH," and "Broke ISH." We called our AI episode "Robots Taking Over This ISH." At first, we struggled to figure out how to start the episode, given how unapproachable the topic of AI can be. The *Adult ISH* team came up with the idea of having Merk and Nyge do their usual greetings at the top of the show in voices manipulated by AI so that from the episode's first moments, listeners would experience an example of how AI can twist our normal realities. Then with their characteristic banter, Merk and Nyge laid the groundwork for the rest of the episode:

Merk: We've already been using AI all the time whether we know it or not. It's technology like that that makes stuff like Siri and self-driving cars possible. . . . Some of it is actually pretty cool!

Nyge: Yeah, but what about machines taking over human jobs? And privacy issues? I also read that facial recognition sucks for Black, Brown, and genderqueer people, and yet some police departments are using it for profiling.

Merk: Ooh, that explains a lot of systematic problems we have.

Nyge: Yeah, and what in heck are these AI robots even learning from us? And what are they going to do with what they learn? I don't know. Again, that's why these robots are taking over this *ISH*.

Merk: And we're gonna get into all of that today by exploring pros and deeply rooted cons we have about interacting with this kind of technology as young adults.[1]

For one segment of the episode, Merk and Nyge took up the topic of "uncanny valley." It's a term that Japanese roboticist Masahiro Mori came up with to describe the reactions people have to humanlike robots—that creepy sensation of encountering something that's *almost* a person, but not quite. Mori called this type of uncanny sensation a "valley" because using a scale from negative to positive emotions, he had graphed people's responses to various types of machines approximating human qualities. He found a deep dip in the graph right at the point where the likeness got really close but not all the way to matching an actual sentient being. The *Adult ISH* team invited YR Media's interactive designer, Marjerrie, a recent art school graduate, onto the show. The idea was for her to run through a series of uncanny valley scenarios to spark reflections on how the scenarios made them feel, and more fundamentally, about the relationship between technology and human expression. Here's how Marj introduced the third scenario:

Marjerrie: I do have another scenario for you all. Nyge, I hear you love poetry.

Nyge: Yup.

Marjerrie: Let's say your cohost, Merk, invites you to a local open mic event. A poetry slam event that she found through Instagram. . . . So while at the event, there's one poem you really, really liked. You talk to the poet at the end of the night who confesses he actually didn't write the poem. It was actually a bot who wrote it.

Nyge: A fraud![2]

Marj then read two poems to Merk and Nyge, one composed by a bot, and the other by a human, and she asked them to guess which was which. Merk guessed wrong, and Nyge got it right. About the AI-generated verses, Marj explained that a Duke University undergrad wrote the code that created the poem back in 2010. "It was actually accepted by Duke literary press without editors knowing a bot wrote it," she said, "So it's been published!" Their energetic on-air discussion surfaced deep questions about the limits of machine-made art and implications of its proliferation, especially as advances in technology have made it harder and harder to know if a poem, painting, or piece of music is the product of an algorithm or an artist's mind.

Coding for Creative Expression

Just as Marj and the *Adult ISH* team sensed that a story about the boundary between technology and human artistry would be a strong way to open their episode, we lead with the same example here for our discussion of coding for creative expression. In this chapter, we explore the ways in which young people use computational thinking to produce something we typically associate with a characteristically human capacity: expressing oneself through art.

So far we have looked at interactive projects that build insight, community, and connection as well as public accountability. Creative expression has been a factor across all the digital products we've considered through those lenses. We talked about the decidedly counterstereotypical graphics of *West Side Stories*, nuanced illustrations for *Little Rock Nine Live*, and the design and photography of *What If You Ruled the School's Dress Code?* So we have already seeded the notion of coding for creative expression. We have seen young people tapping their imaginations, sourcing from art worlds for inspiration and elements to feature in their interactives, and exercising technical skills grounded in the arts—from color and composition theory, to the use of scoring and soundtracks—to deepen their own learning and heighten the impact of their products. In this chapter, we focus even further on the intersection between computation and imagination through a set of interactive projects that all take up themes related to AI.

We situate our approach in a field of study and practice that is framed through the STEAM moniker. Around the same time that we were developing the projects highlighted here, YR Media joined an international research team called Science Learning Plus, dedicated to the study of out-of-school learning at the intersection of science and art. We are indebted to those colleagues in our conceptualization of coding for creative expression, including our ambivalence toward the framework of STEAM itself.[3] Typically, STEAM puts the arts in service of the more highly prized domain of STEM, as suggested by the insertion of a mere "A" alongside four science disciplines. Those other fields derive greater status than the arts through their association with well-compensated career pathways and their perceived role driving national economic competitiveness. While reducing creative expression to a means for learning STEM denigrates the arts, this approach also falls short in a less obvious way. By hoarding creativity for the arts alone, we fail to recognize the critical role it plays as a practice crucial to any robust practice of STEM too.[4]

As we have argued alongside our Science Learning Plus colleagues, we are especially drawn to STEAM approaches that combine practices from the arts and STEM fields in ways that mutually enrich both. The arts and STEM have much in common. Both involve exploring, meaning making, and critiquing.[5] Efforts that lean more heavily toward the arts may express meaning through open-ended symbols, whereas in STEM we may be more likely to form arguments using data. When we carry out STEAM activities, we encourage young people to create products that account for both symbolic resonance and data rigor. With respect to the process of critique, artists and STEM practitioners build on established theories and methodologies—sometimes grounding their efforts in those traditions, and at other times deliberately defying them to arrive at something new. In the arts and STEM, we release work to the public. We might seek different outcomes for our audiences—to inform them, move them, delight them, upset them, spark them to action, and so on. But regardless of the objective, when we produce digital media that draws nimbly from the arts and STEM, we are better positioned to achieve whatever impact we seek than if we relied on just one "side" or the other, and we expand the range in points of entry for contributors with diverse interests.

Because working at the intersection of diverse fields opens up new possibilities for expression, the STEAM framework has the potential to unlock an imaginative space where we start to conceive of the world "as if it were otherwise," where "life could be lived differently."[6] Within this space, we can deploy the tools of the arts and STEM to make moves—imperfect, incomplete moves, but necessary moves nonetheless—to help bring that better world and more fully realized self into existence.[7]

When we center our coding efforts in a process of creative expression, we engage in a "practice of possibility" that enables young people "to envision what they want to become, and who they want to be."[8]

The expressive dimension of this work can be personal, when individual young people find voice for their unique experiences. Maybe they're alone in a sound booth mixing a beat or drawing on a tablet in their bedrooms late into the night. Expression can also be collective, when producers tap shared ideas and identities, sampling from earlier artists or traditions to convey a community truth. As evident in prior chapters, creative expression in the context of YR Media doesn't overly valorize genius originality. Yes, we push ourselves to tell fresh stories and spur new, rich conversations through our stories, but not at the expense of honoring and ethically drawing from prior efforts. We have seen in earlier chapters the ways in which young people find inspiration in film references (like the movie *Clueless* for the *Dress Code* project) or modify open-source code (like the tutorial we used as a basis for *West Side Stories*). The inheritance of prior creativity is a boon for contemporary makers in the arts and STEM. Creative expression is grounded in the concrete, experimenting with tactile and digital materials, designing prototypes and polishing finished products. And yet we also embrace the ambiguous and uncertain as we grapple with problems that we ourselves define, where there exists no "right answer" to the questions we pose. When we are coding for creative expression, we experience heightened attunement to the details of our environments—the objects, people, and ideas we encounter. "Creative expression is rooted in the capacities for observation, discovery, imagination, and courage. It wakes us up, challenges us, and enriches all of life."[9]

Can You Teach AI to Dance? Where It Began

When we're coding for creative expression, we have to start somewhere, and like so many YR Media projects, this one began with a provocation.[10] One day in 2018, the interactive team's cofounder and leader, Asha, presented the young people with a surprising piece of information about a platform, Spotify, they used every day. All the young people were familiar with how Spotify worked. None of them knew about a hidden ranking system that categorizes the site's tens of millions of songs. While not visible in the user interface, a range of scores, including a "danceability" rating, is algorithmically assigned to every song on the platform. As soon as Asha revealed this algorithm on Spotify's back-end application programming interface, the youth team immediately began testing and exploring how it worked.

"So then we started to experiment," explained Shaundra. "Going on Spotify, and listening to a song and guessing its danceability, and us being shocked about the danceability score. And then that went to us wanting to create a website or an interactive about our difference in ratings of a song."

"Yeah," added her peer, Micah. "We kind of began questioning the authority of the Spotify rating, and what it meant and how it influenced people."

The youth team members were immediately engaged. They rapidly progressed from being shocked about a feature of technology they unknowingly *used* to envisioning a digital product they could *create*. From these first moments of contemplating the project, the young people called out issues of authority and influence. Already they were interrogating the power of tech in general and AI specifically to shape a deeply personal aspect of their lives: their taste in music. Driving their production process was a series of questions. How were these ratings produced? By whom? How are they used? What are they missing? What assumptions do they reveal? How are these judgments about a song's quality different from our own?

Data Science, Computational Thinking, and Critical Cultural Analysis

"I think it started out . . . as questioning the Spotify algorithm. . . . But now it's about comparing and . . . learning about AI . . . and how it applies to us. Because you think about AI as like this big futuristic thing, but you realize Spotify, which you use every day, is using it too," said Shaundra.

"It is often worrisome to me how heavy-handed the ability of taking control of other people's wants is getting with big tech," Danny added. "And I think it's very important to the average user to understand that that's happening." Here Danny is starting to see a role for himself and his colleagues on the interactive team. They'll need to understand the technology and its connection to big tech enough to create a product that sparks those insights in others. His concern about people's "wants" is worth paying special attention to in the context of creative expression. He's beginning to scope out a project that aims to preserve the "average user's" agency in making aesthetic judgments, even with an AI operating behind the scenes.

In order to go beyond these initial questions, the young people had to gather some basic information. How exactly does Spotify code and score songs for danceability, and based on what data? The team researched the origins of this feature in a start-up company that Spotify acquired that had developed a system for rating songs for qualities including "loudness," "speechiness," and "instrumentalness." The team poured over a spreadsheet displaying factors that the algorithm took into account in assigning the danceability score (see figure 6.1).

Next, the team members played with the data and experimented with ways to visualize it. In pairs and small groups, they wireframed various designs for an interactive "explainer" that would reveal how the AI-powered rating system operated. They had to come up with a

	song	artist	danceability	energy	key	loudness	mode	speechiness	acousticness
1	I Fink U freeky	Die Antwoord	0.844	0.751	6	-6.5	1	0.223	0.0292
2	MIC Drop		0.667	0.889	6	-4.851	1	0.0918	0.00912
3	Take It All		0.731	0.503	10	-13.136	1	0.0377	0.108
4	Big Bank	YG	0.743	0.339	1	-7.678	1	0.409	0.00582
5	Run the World	Beyonce	0.733	0.899	0	-4.237	1	0.143	0.00496
6	Toxic	Britney Spears	0.774	0.838	5	-3.914	0	0.114	0.0249
7	D.A.N.C.E		0.613	0.962	6	5.07	0	0.278	0.034
8	Ode to victory		0.514	0.632	2	-6.305	1	0.0501	0.208
9	Ball	T.I.	0.772	0.885	1	-4.736	1	0.0847	0.193
10	Fatty Boom Boom	Die Antwoord	0.833	0.85	2	-4.964	1	0.211	0.151

Figure 6.1
Spreadsheet to track factors in the Spotify algorithm.

concept that went beyond a static story reporting out the facts. Because we work in the interactive department, their designs needed to invite users into a hands-on, digitally enabled experience. The youth team members wanted their audience to delve into some of the same questions they were intrigued by when they first learned about the danceability score, and thus participate in and not merely witness the meaning-making process. This meant that in addition to producing analysis and designs, the young people would need to learn enough about coding—HTML, CSS, and JavaScript—to develop an intuitive, illuminating user experience.

"Because sometimes I see something and I'm like, 'Oh, that's just there and that just is,'" said Shaundra, acknowledging the resigned stance she often takes with respect to technology—or at least did before beginning to make her own. But "then you can start to question it, and understand what they are doing and how they're affecting us."

Danny built on her point: "What I also noticed is that artificial intelligence or machine learning algorithms tend to be based on the designer's point of view." He referenced a news story he'd read a few months prior reporting that Amazon had tested a hiring algorithm, "and I think it was biased against a group of people. . . . And of course the study group put together by Amazon was like, 'Oh! We don't know why that happened.' But it happened because the statistics that it learned from came from you guys!"

Here Danny calls out the companies and designers who fail to factor the full range of human experiences into the technology they create, developing systems that reflect and reify inequalities related to race and other variables. Underlying this point is an even more fundamental awareness: there are people behind the systems and algorithms that structure our experiences. The young people were beginning to recognize themselves as possessing the capacity as well as responsibility to design systems in dynamic and critical ways. So while this chapter is focused on the importance of creative expression, we see the role of developing a critical consciousness in all the products we create.

Playful Design for Profound Learning

Following initial ideation and research, the youth team designed an early prototype to visualize the danceability data in the form of bubbles of various mathematically determined sizes clustered in ways to show how various songs compared. In the screenshot below, the displayed data show differences between Britney Spears and BTS, for example (see figure 6.2).

As the young people continued to develop, share, critique, and iterate on possible designs, they eventually refined and narrowed their scope to a "minimum viable product." YR Media editors enlisted a young writer, Deb Raji, who was studying CS in college and has gone on to coauthor some of the most groundbreaking studies we have on bias in AI, to compose an article that would introduce the interactive.[11] The written piece would provide a basic explanation of how AI works and contextualize it within wider themes. Meanwhile, the Oakland-based youth team went to work designing a gamelike experience to invite users to compare their danceability scores with Spotify's, tapping a colleague from the music department to put together a playlist of

Figure 6.2
Early prototype to display the danceability data.

WHAT'S DANCEABLE? YOUR TURN!

Figure 6.3
Screen capture of *Can You Teach AI to Dance?* interactive with a song and comparison of your danceability rating alongside Spotify's, with accompanying GIFs.

songs from a range of genres that, to his ears, spanned the danceability spectrum.

A key technical feature of the final product illuminates the youth designers' emerging CCE. When a user listens to one of the songs on the playlist, they are invited to score that track for danceability on a scale of one to ten. But in addition to displaying the number, the interactive serves up a GIF that essentially "translates" the number into a short video of a popular culture figure. Pick a low score, like two, and the GIF shows Rihanna rolling her eyes. A higher score of nine gets you Beyoncé surrounded by a bunch of dancers doing intricate choreography. It's a playful feature with profound meaning through which the young people converted an otherwise-dry quantification into a culturally specific moving image, implicitly pushing back against the reduction of songs they love to numerical values.

Members of the youth team identified the GIFs as an example of how their voices and decision-making were reflected in the interactive:

Shaundra: As you slide along the slider, the GIFs change. . . . I tried my hardest with picking the GIFs that matched the numbers as much as possible because I feel like that really can tell the user the weight of that number.

Researcher: The GIF is more meaningful than the number?

Shaundra: Yeah. Because with just the slider, and without the GIFs, I feel like it's going to be kind of hard for you to rate something. I feel like the GIFs add an extra touch so you know exactly what our four means instead of just having a number there.

Micah: Yeah. You got to choose all the GIFs. Also, like, all the ideas, like the slider, where the buttons are placed, came from somebody. Because we each started to design our own thing and made it—compiled all the best ideas into one thing.

The team members selected and organized the proposed GIFs in a spreadsheet used to inform their design choices (see figure 6.4). Populating this data set entailed the mix of computational, imaginative, and culturally relevant thinking that went into the making of *Can You Teach AI to Dance?*

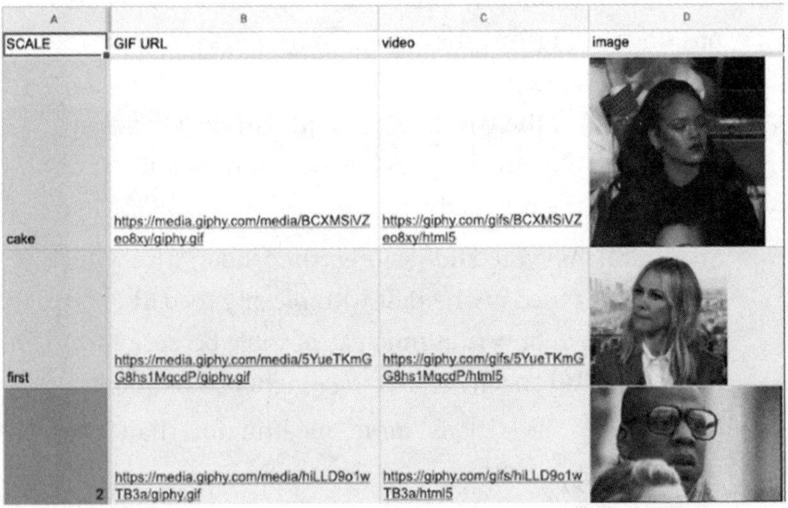

Figure 6.4
Spreadsheet of GIFs for the danceability scale.

Expression as a Response to Technical Challenges

Throughout this project, the young people were as tuned into their learning process as they were into the details of their finished product. Inevitably, as they developed the interactive, they would make mistakes, such as misspelling a word in their code. "I remember Danny and I, like if you wrote something wrong, like the entire creation would be upside down and backward. And it's like, 'Oh my God, I broke everything!'" said Micah. Working through their errors, however, offered important learning opportunities.

"You have to find the mistake," said Micah. "It's so frustrating because you're like, 'That little tiny thing [had] such a big impact.'"

They remembered their instructor Asha's admonition. She didn't like it when they said, "I broke it."

"Because not only was it obviously very frustrating to her to hear it 'broke' but she also put a very strong emphasis on debugging and reading your code," said Danny.

"Yeah," Micah added. "It was really important to learn how to debug it yourself too."

"When you do say, 'It's broke,' it is vague," Danny went on. "It does kind of provide a vague sense of brokenness." Danny's talking about something technical here—the process of debugging a coded work in progress—but the poetry of his words points to a deeper significance. He credits his mentor, Asha, for helping him to reframe a potentially overwhelming and incapacitating "vague sense of brokenness" into a temporary state that he is empowered to change. "It's like, 'Well, what did you do last?'" Danny continued, playing out the logic that he had learned from Asha, encouraging the team to "walk backward" through their process and notice the steps they'd taken. "It not only pushes them through a backward train of thought where they watch themselves and watch what they did, what they coded, and see why it stopped making something work. But it also allows them to take time to . . . figure out what's wrong. Stopping could take minutes, hours, days. But eventually, you get it." We asked Asha about why this approach was so important to her:

> You weren't allowed to say 'It's broken' because that's not descriptive. It does not help me help you. And it's a little bit defeatist. Like, 'Oh, it's broken. What can I do about that?' And I think that you can fix your problems. . . . It's a new opportunity to make it a little bit better. For young people, once they had that experience of 'It didn't go the way I planned, and I pivoted or I fixed it,' people would be so hyped. . . . And then they would be excited to help their friends or to tell them, 'You can do it too.' And my hope is that they were able to apply that to the rest of their life, like things aren't gonna go the way you want, but that doesn't mean it's broken.

This is a small-scale version of the practice of possibility that we talked about at the beginning of this chapter. Within the moment-to-moment effort to make their thing work, Danny and his colleagues are reenvisioning what they are capable of, what problem-solving options are at their disposal, "what they want to become, and who they want to be."[12]

Further, the process that Danny and Asha describe captures the heightened attunement we see again and again in projects that integrate computation, critical analysis, and creative expression. The young people bring the same self-scrutiny and rigor to deciding exactly the right GIF to represent, say, a three on the danceability scale as they do to composing exactly the right line of code to power the feature they have in mind. When their efforts don't immediately work as they expected, they make adjustments to improve the product's quality or usability. In this respect, the thoughtful curation of GIFs is not more or less important than the code that runs the interactive. Neither is elevated above the other, but instead they work in tandem to engage the user. Through design cycles, the creators gain knowledge and confidence to produce more dynamic media, and build toward a fuller sense of the possible future they can be a part of making.

Erase Your Face

A second AI project that manifests coding for creative expression is *Erase Your Face*.[13] We got started on this one about a year after *Can You Teach AI to Dance?* The youth team members took inspiration from an article that their colleague Marjerrie wrote for YR Media called

"Your Guide to Anti-Surveillance Fashion."[14] When she wasn't teaching in the interactive department or creating design assets for the newsroom, Marjerrie—an emerging writer and artist in her own right—occasionally contributed tech stories to YR Media's website. In this piece, she explored various artists' experiments with garments, accessories, and other style moves that would allow people to evade AI facial recognition. For example, back in 2010, an NYU grad student created a tool kit called "CZ Dazzle" that used hair extensions and makeup as camouflage (see figure 6.5).

Marjerrie wrote about another arts-based experiment, the "CHBL Jammer Coat," which was made of fabric that blocked radio waves to shield the wearer against tracking

A variety of looks styled for a Coreana Museum of Art workshop that utilizes CV Dazzle anti-facial recognition methods. (Photos: Cha Hyun Seok)

Figure 6.5
Image displaying CV Dazzle antifacial recognition methods.
Photo credit: <Tech Camouflage: Anti-Face Detection Makeup Workshop>. Organized by the Coreana Museum of Art, Seoul. Inspired by Adam Harvey's Project, CV Dazzle. Photo by Cha Hyun Seok.

devices. She described a line of garments called "REAL-FACE Glamoflauge," which were covered with celebrity faces to confuse Facebook's tagging mechanism. The youth team was especially fascinated by the artist Leo Salvaggio's work. He offered up a 3D-printed photorealistic mask of his own face for others to use so that anyone could "read" to surveillance systems as Salvaggio instead of themselves.

Understanding Facial Recognition's Foundations

"Your Guide to Anti-Surveillance Fashion" was one of several news stories and research investigations that young people took cues from to build their understanding of AI facial recognition technologies as well as find inspiration for what they would create. The team members explored why and how facial recognition systems often depend on algorithms that exhibit bias relative to race and gender, with the highest error rates among female and darker-skinned groups.[15] They discovered a sharp uptick in the number of misuses of public surveillance systems developed by large, influential companies and made available to law enforcement agencies. The nonconsensual use of publicly accessible images, such as drivers licenses, mug shots, and photos on social media, by law enforcement agencies increases the likelihood that Black and Brown people will be wrongfully implicated in criminal offenses.

To further understand the racial context for surveillance systems and potential for bias in AI more broadly, we drew from a growing body of research in STEM education identifying best practices for teaching AI, including the AI4K12 model that offers five "big ideas" in AI (perception, representation and reasoning, learning, natural interaction, and societal impact).[16] We also partnered with two high school students working with a team at Stanford d.school to interview University of Texas at Austin professor Simone Browne, who wrote *Dark Matters: On the Surveillance of Blackness*, and included excerpts of that interview in our final post. What began with artistic experiments quickly led the youth team to uncover the troubling implications of the unchecked use of facial recognition technologies.

"Everyday our privacy is being imposed on. There is not much you can do," said one member of the youth team. They remarked that facial recognition was being used indiscriminately in public infrastructure, even though explicit consent is typically required to use their likenesses in other areas of their lives. They shared these kinds of observations with Marjerrie as they worked on their design: "They were comparing it at some point to the media release forms that they usually have to sign at the beginning of each school year. They sign off to do that, but you didn't sign off for your face to be used in some sort of facial recognition system. And so there was a lot of conversation about permission, especially if it's their own face." Because so many of the young people on the interactive team belonged to one or more of the identity groups that facial recognition technologies render unrecognizable, feelings of anger and fear further motivated them to create an interactive that shook their users into awareness of the risks of this particular form of emerging technology if not implemented with strong ethical standards. Through research and reflection, the young people considered how to create a product that could draw attention to companies, programmers, and products that contribute to systems that perpetuate bias.

Hands-on Design to Understand Technological Systems
With the support of their professional designer and developer colleagues, the youth team members deepened their understanding of facial recognition through a series of exploratory, hands-on experiments using physical materials, centering imagination as a way to structure their learning process and project design. Marjerrie brought in construction paper, foil, paints, and magazine cutouts, which the young people then used to collage into strategic masks with the intention of finding ways to defy detection by facial recognition technologies. They tested each unique creation on their own faces using a tool called Amazon Rekognition, a publicly available facial recognition service that provides a percentage called a "similarity score" to show how closely each obscured image resembles a corresponding unaltered photo (see figure 6.6). The young people cheered each time that their creation resulted in less than an 80 percent match, the benchmark set by the Amazon Rekognition developer guide. Wins were hard to come

Face comparison

Compare faces to see how closely they match based on a similarity percentage.

Reference face

Comparison faces

Done with the demo?
Learn more

▾ Results

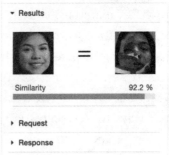

Similarity   92.2 %

▸ Request

▸ Response

Figure 6.6
Experimenting with facial recognition software.

by, and the students expressed awe and astonishment when their faces remained detectable despite their elaborate masks. "I was shocked at how hard it was to not recognize your face. Every time, it got my face," said Stacey.

The similarity score offered insights into the most effective materials and placements to trick the algorithm and evade recognition. Marjerrie reflected on how the young people developed "a critical lens and set of working theories through hands-on design."[17]

The interactive team members used the insights from their own experimentation process as the basis of a project design that would allow users to create and test techniques that circumvent surveillance and facial recognition. At the same time that they developed that interactive user experience, the young people worked with the project's lead producer, Nimah, in consultation with AI experts to write the story that established the context of facial recognition as technology that is already shaping young people's lives, whether they know it or not. We seized on the coronavirus pandemic, which was surging at the time, to establish the topic's relevance and what was at stake in the introduction to *Erase Your Face*:

> In the grand scheme of frustrations related to the pandemic, this one's small: you hold your phone up so Face ID can unlock it. You sit there for a few seconds before realizing, oh right, you've got a mask on! Your phone doesn't recognize you. The reason? For facial recognition to work, it has to be able to detect what makes your face unique. The technology turns that information into numbers. Yep, hate to break it to

you, but each of our lovely faces can be represented
through something like a massive spreadsheet filled
with digits. Meanwhile, long before you're sitting there
trying in vain to get past your phone's pesky password
screen, tech companies have already converted millions
and millions of other faces into number sets to create
a humongous database for comparison. If your mask
blocks enough of your distinctive facial information,
even the best algorithms in the world can't figure out
who you are.[18]

This notion of what it takes for technology to "figure out who you are" became the basis for the final version of *Erase Your Face*. The team members wanted to
emulate the same experience they had achieved using
art materials to collage over their actual faces. But how
could they make that process digital? They landed on the
idea of inviting users to upload or select a photo, and use
a drawing tool that Danny and Radamés, the team's lead
developer, created to scribble over the portrait. Then users
could feed their altered faces into the Amazon Rekognition tool to get their own "similarity scores" in order to
see if they'd managed to bypass recognition. Here's how
we set it up in the finished post (see figure 6.7): "We
wanted to give you a chance to try defying recognition
yourself. Using your cursor or finger, select a color and
draw over the provided image. Employing a service
called Amazon Rekognition, your drawing will be tested
against a sea of other A.I.-generated faces to see if the
software can still make a match, despite your attempt
to go incognito."

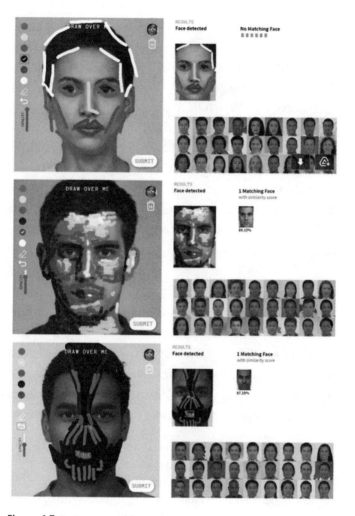

Figure 6.7
Screen capture from our *Erase Your Face* interactive.

Each step along the way in building this final product raised complex questions. For example, what photos to use? At first, we considered developing a feature where users could pick one of their own images. But we realized, if the whole point of the interactive was to get users to think critically about how legible they wanted to be to detection, then the last requirement that we would want to build into the experience would be the mandate to share your own image. The alternative we came up with was to invite users to choose portraits from a database that Radamés and Marjerrie found containing more than two million AI-generated faces.

Youth Privacy / Youth Agency

In the making of *Erase Your Face*, CCE formed the conditions that helped young people establish their own creative agency despite growing tech encroachment into practically every aspect of our lives. Radamés reflected on how young people applied their emerging skills in design, research, data, and coding in a process that centered their creative imaginations:

> That's why art is very interesting because of our creativity and ability to understand what the computer cannot. Just playing with different colors. . . . It's a slightly minor detail that makes a big difference that would have a lot of impact on the system. I think that's the space for art to be open, to be playful. The system's trying to find some logical patterns based on what it has learned, but then suddenly what emerges from that interaction is something that only [we] can interpret, and get some beauty, and have fun.

Like *Can You Teach AI to Dance?*, *Erase Your Face* is an exercise in reimagining possible futures. Taken together, the two projects offer up experiences where we can experiment with defying pervasive technologies' terms. We can expose and challenge a hidden algorithm designed to shape our musical tastes. We can see what it feels like to dodge surveillance software that turns us into data points without necessarily obtaining our informed consent, serving our needs, or seeing us for who we are. Neither project dismantles the systems that produce these features, nor does either even necessarily advocate for opting out of the tools or platforms that use this technology. Rather, these interactives shine a light on aspects of our digital world that otherwise exist in black boxes, penetrable only by those with access to the backrooms (and back ends) where these tools are made. In both cases, the young people grapple with quantitative data, like scores measuring "danceability" and "similarity." These numbers assign values—both literal and figurative—in ways that are not always transparent, representative, or fair. And with each project, young people used creative expression to find meaning in those quantitative data, bringing numbers alive through animated GIFs or digital renderings that revealed their significance, and indexed a sense of belonging through shared cultural references that resonate especially with communities too often misrepresented and ill served by tech.

In the early stages of their projects, the young people expressed strong emotions. The hubris of a music platform that dares to claim it can score a song's danceability using algorithms alone, and the profound flaws of facial recognition tools that institutions including law enforcement agencies use despite widely reported bias—these are some of the revelations that inspired young people to learn about AI. Over time, they developed sufficient technical know-how, creative engagement, and critical curiosity about the implications of these systems to produce their own digital products that sparked new understandings in themselves and their audiences.

7
We Code for Joy and Hope

As with all the chapters in this book, when we got started on this one, we queried journal databases for relevant articles. It was not the first time that we've been struck by how much you can learn from an academic literature search before reading a single publication. What we found was not especially surprising but striking nonetheless.

First, our queries related to joy and hope in CS education yielded far fewer results than prior searches for our other chapters—about one-quarter the number, once we eliminated the name "Joy" as an author. Second, the titles that did surface tended to focus on young children, which makes sense. Most preschool and elementary teachers will tell you that cultivating joy is critical to their teaching repertoire. When it comes to high school–aged young people, it's harder to know how to make space for joy in the academic context or recognize it. Adolescents don't always show joy in ways adults can understand or see as valid, especially when additional cultural divides compound generational ones. And too often for teens and young adults, pleasure is set up in opposition to privileged educational outcomes like academic achievement, skills mastery, and pathways into higher education and employment. What we too often miss is the critical role that joy plays in realizing these outcomes. Joy and hope can enable students to take risks, overcome challenges, pursue goals, and develop a positive attitude toward learning.[1] When well-designed, culturally relevant lessons connect joy to hope, engagement deepens and expands, and students begin to see their work as part of a bigger, broader effort to build a better world.

We are not alone in our growing attunement to joy and hope in CS education. Entire programs are springing up that center emotion and play, even for teens and young adults, and these developments are encouraging. The Beauty and Joy in Computing initiative at the University of California at Berkeley, for example, is grounded in what Seymour Papert called the "hard fun" of constructing through code.[2] Emerging research is drawing a through line from joy to justice. In 2021, the two of us were part of a session at the American Education Research Association called Humanizing Computer Science Education. Led by Mia Shaw, Yasmin Kafai, and Christina Gardner-McCune, contributors to the panel presented a range of studies at the intersection of technology and culture. All of us contextualized our research and practice against the backdrop of the systemic problems that plague our field. We cited data showing that Black students were less likely than their white peers to attend schools that offer dedicated CS classes.[3] We called out education, child welfare, and criminal justice systems for continuing to use machine learning tools that perpetuate algorithmic bias. We predicted that these biases would only get worse if we don't make radical changes to CS curriculum and pedagogy.

And yet the papers presented on that panel took the problems troubling our field as points of departure rather than critical ends in themselves. We framed studies that heeded sociologist Ruha Benjamin's call to "remember to imagine and craft the worlds you cannot live without, just as you dismantle the ones you cannot live within."[4] Organizers, artists, and theorists with the Movement for Black Lives have been modeling this crucial work of crafting imagined worlds that care for and cultivate Black joy. So have Afrofuturists, who set the cultural expressions of the African diaspora in relationship to the technologies of today and possible tomorrows.[5] Our efforts and those of our copresenters are profoundly indebted to these frameworks, embodied by the multidimensional definition of joy that Bettina Love offers in her groundbreaking book *We Want to Do More than Survive*:

> I am talking about joy that originates in resistance, joy that is discovered in making a way out of no way, joy that is uncovered when you know how to love yourself and others, joy that comes from releasing pain, joy that is generated in music and art that puts words and/or images to your life's greatest challenges and pleasures, and joy in teaching from a place of resistance, agitation, purpose, justice, love, and mattering.[6]

Teaching from the kind of place that Love describes was a theme across the session. Authors explored how Black middle schoolers developed games through which they established their "rightful presence" in the world of CS and beyond, Black girls integrated e-textiles and augmented reality video effects into dance, and a multiracial group of young people reimagined dominant narratives through computational quilts.[7] In all cases, joy and hope were key. Taken together, these and related studies establish promising new directions for CS where the very students most underrepresented in and betrayed by the field reimagine teaching and learning in ways that celebrate community splendor along with the capacity to take delight in one's own goodness, the well-being of others, and the difference code can make.[8]

When they're coding for joy, youth creators work through struggles while developing new stories that honor their histories and shared experiences, and speak truth to power. Coding for joy is making "a way out of no way," bringing levity and humor to exhausting work. It surfaces in the satisfaction of overcoming daunting computational, journalistic, and aesthetic challenges to arrive at the next stage of development. Coding for joy is passing off parts of a project to trusted team members and getting back a better-designed, more efficiently engineered product that still feels like it belongs to you. Coding for joy builds features that highlight community resilience. It comes in the moment of publication, when the work is finally done. And it extends through the project's digital afterlife, when others start to engage with and share it—especially when those others are people with the most at stake in the issues that the project explores. There can even be moments of joy when audiences take issue with our more provocative stories because sometimes the first sign that our work is gaining traction is evidence that it's making the right people mad.

Fundamentally, coding for joy is using computational thinking to develop stories and tools that produce a more humanizing world. "The greatest casualty of trauma is not only depression and emotional scars," wrote youth development researcher and theorist Shawn Ginwright, "but also the loss of the ability to dream and imagine another way of living." CCE counters that loss by cultivating joy and hope, as young people encode stories that enable them to "envision what they want to become, and who they want to be."[9]

Affirmations, Icons, and Ancestors

The themes we raise here pick up threads that have run through all the chapters of this book. Across the projects we have already looked at, we have seen evidence of young people coding joy and hope into their creations. When YR Media's case manager advised the makers of *Mood Ring* against classifying tough emotions like anger and sadness as "negative," the team members revised their design to ensure that the app affirmed future users who were experiencing those feelings rather than risk driving them further into despair. That update was an exercise in hope as a dimension of CCE. And then Nala took the approach further by insisting that the team add affirmations so that each time users opened *Mood Ring*, they'd receive a message that would make them feel less alone and more prepared to face their day. Even the functionality that the team added that allowed users to choose more than one emoji when tracking their mental states exemplified coding for joy. This new feature allowed for shades of "excitement" or "motivation" to mix with feelings like "sadness," "irritation," or a sense of being "overwhelmed."

For *Your Queer Rights*, the team members were already fairly far along in the project when they realized that an app so heavily focused on the pain and injustice of anti-LGBTQ+ discrimination needed a new feature. So they updated the interface with the photos and bios of queer icons like Marsha P. Johnson, who fought to include trans people under the umbrella of gay rights; Lou Sullivan, credited with distinguishing between sexual orientation and gender identity; writers James Baldwin and Alison Bechdel; prison abolitionist Patrisse Cullors; and director and activist Janet Mock. Given that the app was designed to provide resources to users who felt they were being discriminated against, humiliated, or threatened on the basis of their LGBTQ+ identity, the creators knew that they would be catching young people at a vulnerable moment. The app's developers had lived through such moments themselves. They understood the power of an image and life story appearing at that very second, with the click of a button on their phones, to remind users of the artists and activists who had fought for their rights and embodied hope for safe, full, creative lives.

Coding for joy and hope cuts across YR Media's interactive portfolio in less obvious ways as well. When Desean created those vibrant digital portraits of the Little Rock Nine, he brought new life to their stories, and found joy in linking their courage and power to his own. "It's connected to my history," he said of the story he was helping to craft. "These are like my ancestors." In tying his collective past to the future of racial equity in US schools, which was the objective of the *LR9LIVE* project, Desean brings to mind the legacy of feminist educator and scholar Anna Julia Cooper. At the turn of the twentieth century, she wrote, "We look back, not to become inflated with conceit because of the depths from which we have arisen, but that we may learn wisdom from the experience. We look within that we may gather together once more our forces, and, by improved and more practical methods, address ourselves to the tasks before us."[10] Cooper lays groundwork for the idiom within ethnic studies that says, "Know history, know self. No history, no self." Knowing self is one of the most fundamental ways to defy unjust institutions that put young people at odds with themselves, their histories, and their cultural wealth.[11] Defying those dehumanizing forces through knowledge of self and community is a story of coding for hope.

Projects like *Can You Teach AI to Dance?* and *Erase Your Face* manifest coding for joy and hope in a different way. These interactives apply playful frames to their hard-hitting critiques of AI's flaws and the dread many of us experience contemplating what its unfettered proliferation could mean. You listen to a song from Spotify, rate it for danceability, and then see which GIF—Beyoncé dancing or Steph Curry nodding—the designers chose to embody your score in comparison to the one Spotify generated via machine learning. Or you scribble all over a face of your choosing to see just what combination of lines, colors, and patterns will work to obscure the face enough to avoid recognition by AI. Again and again we saw *Erase Your Face* users cheer when they finally "beat" the machine. In these ways, YR Media's designers used code and other tools to produce story worlds where critique and delight, struggle and pleasure, injustice and resilience, could coexist. In so doing, they found a place for themselves in the actual worlds they've inherited and are working to remake.

We want to call out the fact that actually developing these joy-enabling features takes work—technical work. Coding for joy and hope requires more than espousing this approach as an ideal. Making good on that commitment means dedicating development cycles to these dimensions of the work just as one would for any other product feature. Operating in the realm of joy and hope doesn't set us apart from algorithmic problem-solving. The opposite is true. To create the functionality that serves users the affirmations, emoji, icons, digital illustrations, GIFs, and other interactive experiences we have just highlighted across YR Media's portfolio of projects, young people had to translate their vision into code. They needed to identify and investigate problems, set goals, develop strategies to achieve them, carry out research, collect and analyze various types of data, use a range of technical tools and languages, and leverage expertise in themselves and others.

Program leaders partnering with young people need to be willing to allocate the necessary time, care, and labor to engineer joy and hope into the user experience, without sacrificing those same qualities in our learning environments. This imperative is rooted, once again, in Paolo Freire's notion of praxis, a blend of theory and practice that grounds emancipatory work. In a conversation with Freire published in the 1990, Myles Horton, the legendary popular educator and social justice leader, spoke of the dynamic between conceptualization and concrete engagement, thinking and making. "I can say that theory didn't come out of my head," he wrote. "That came out of action."[12]

We Literally Redrew Our Community (and You Can Too)

Perhaps no project in YR Media's interactive portfolio captures the praxis of coding for joy and hope more directly than one called *We Literally Redrew Our Community (and You Can Too)*.[13] We developed this project in partnership with Jersey Art Exchange, a media arts and technology nonprofit for teens and young adults in Jersey City, New Jersey. Six young people took the lead on the project. Their idea was to reimagine their town's once-thriving, now-struggling main street, which had been hit hard by "rising rents, $4 coffee shops overrun with hipsters, [and] flipped homes with reclaimed wood fences designed to keep neighbors out." Monticello Avenue had become "a graveyard for small businesses," the young people reported. "Former banks, restaurants, and bodegas with empty windows gather dust and graffiti as they wait to be filled by rich outsiders."[14]

The teen producers didn't have the material resources to dismantle capitalism's most harmful effects and redevelop the business district in real life. What they did possess were the media and technical skills as well as the lived experiences, vision, and creativity to transform their community virtually, using digital tools. Working with YR Media's senior producer, Teresa, the young people gave themselves an assignment: to "draw what our community would look like, if we were in charge. We even imagined the backstories behind the new businesses we want to see."

The team took photos of the defunct and empty storefronts on Monticello Avenue, and then created digital illustrations of businesses that they could see bringing each location back to life. Teresa walked the young people through the process of producing the drawings, and then using an open-source tool, creating an interface with a split-screen vertical slider that allowed users to move between their actual and imagined neighborhood, their present and possible future.

The finished interactive doesn't flinch from the unvarnished emptiness of the "before" images, which convey the deterioration along an avenue where teens used to hang out and experience the dynamic energy of their town. But alongside those sobering images, the creators' alternate realities manifested their refusal to accept what was as what would always be.

The specifics of the team's aesthetics and narratives say a lot about the particular issues causing distress in their community. For example, one slider highlighted the dearth of diverse, healthy food options. It replaced a fast-food restaurant with an "affordable, artistic Japanese spot." The designers created a fictional backstory of two Japanese twin brothers who combined their passion for Japanese street food with artistic interior design to create Jitaku and Kibaku Japanese cuisine. "For $5.99, enjoy a sushi platter of California, spicy tuna, and salmon rolls!" they wrote in speculative promotional materials that they ran alongside the "before" and "after" images.

At 92 Monticello Avenue, the team transformed an empty storefront locked behind metal security doors into LazerRaver, a retro-gaming arcade with laser tag and karaoke for teens. "The only options for teens are sitting around the house, watching Netflix, sleeping, and

Figure 7.1
Screen capture from *We Literally Redrew Our Community (and You Can Too)* slider interactive.

gaming," the young people wrote, explaining their rationale for the arcade. "We imagine a business that would
get teens out of the house in a supervised, healthy environment, where we could socialize in a healthy way
with other teens."

Across the street was another empty storefront that
the designers remade into a shop called Plants and Paws,
where a father-and-daughter team created a "garden and
animal shelter whose number-one goal is to serve the
community."

This one was a multipurpose imagined business,
addressing a combination of issues: stray animals on
the street; pets in need of adoption; the need for a community garden as well as food for homeless shelters and
soup kitchens; and lack of work and community service

Figure 7.2
Screen capture from *We Literally Redrew Our Community (and You Can Too)* slider interactive.

opportunities for tweens and teens in their neighbor-hood. Pets and Paws was a one-stop shop that took "pride in hiring teens to better the community."

Through this interactive, the young people "literally redrew" the symbols of depletion and displacement that dotted a beloved street in their community into hope-ful images of how things could be different. They docu-mented the boarded-up storefronts and tagged-up walls as indicators of the gentrifying neighborhood, yet were not defined by what they had lost. Their CCE can be seen as an exercise in "civic imagination," which forms "a col-lective vision for what a better tomorrow might look like" through story worlds that reframe and have the potential to transform real ones.[15] The producers are developing what Antero Garcia and Nicole Mirra call "speculative civic literacy," through which young people "challenge their positioning as not-yet-citizens" and invent new possibilities for community life on their terms.[16] In the context of this project and YR Media more broadly, young people use the tools of design and computation as instruments of community-based civic reinvention.

The creators of *We Literally Redrew Our Community* were uniquely prepared to envision their neighborhood's imagined future because they held deep knowledge of present-day life there, rooted in the inherited and aspirational capital of prior generations that had battled structures not designed for them.[17] These funds of cultural knowledge were especially evident in one before-and-after slider that the team called "My Island." It featured a revitalized fictional immigrant-run business created by "people who came to this country escaping persecution and hardship."

Figure 7.3
Screen capture from *We Literally Redrew Our Community (and You Can Too)* slider interactive.

Jamal was a chef at storm shelters in the Caribbean during the 2010 magnitude-7 earthquake in Haiti. It was during this catastrophe that he met his current wife, Jasmine, a Haitian caterer who lost her home. Jasmine came back with Jamal, and the two dreamed of opening their own restaurants in the inner city. "My Island" combines age-old Caribbean recipes to ensure the best Caribbean experience in the entire planet! The restaurant's signature dish is the Caribbean Combo, a meal that includes a meat dish, a side, and a home-brewed exotic fruit juice—all for five dollars! Meals include papaya juice, conch fritters, potatoes and plantains, jerk chicken, roti, and curry chicken.

The illustrations and backstories that the young people came up with for this project honor community-sustaining efforts in their neighborhood and the vitality in their cultures and themselves. The project cultivates in its makers the ability to dream, which fosters hopefulness and overall well-being, and sustains young people's motivation to develop and enact strategies to achieve their goals.[18] The future produced by this interactive is responsive to immigrant community members, the health and well-being of people and animals, the importance of diverse and fresh food options, and the human need for reliable and sustainable work.

And the impact of a project like this one doesn't stop with this set of creators. Once published, it serves as a blueprint for young people and adults facing similar struggles elsewhere. Another city might find itself in an earlier phase of housing displacement. Surely that location would face its own cultural, political, economic, and environmental dynamics that may not precisely map onto the ones shaping Monticello Avenue. And yet anyone exploring the interactive could apply its logic to their own neighborhoods. The hopefulness of the creators is not merely performative. Their work reminds audiences to continue the struggle to advocate for the full humanity of communities experiencing dispossession, lighten the load on future generations, and use "any media necessary"— including the medium of code—to create the world they want to see.[19]

Before and After: *In Their Own Words*

We Literally Redrew Our Community (and You Can Too) is a story of before and after. The project's visual design makes that time lapse explicit. It's a satisfying feeling to drag those sliders back and forth, revealing and concealing the paired images that the young people created to capture the dispossession they see in their neighborhood today, and the vitality they can imagine in the future.

As we reflect across the full range of projects we've explored in the book and created over more than ten years at YR Media, we are struck by the extent to which a before-and-after dynamic applies across them all as an underlying story of transformation. It shows up in different ways. *West Side Stories* looks at what one Oakland neighborhood was like before gentrification intensified, and what the community is like now and going forward, for longtime residents and newcomers. *Your Queer Rights* turns back toward LGBTQ+ icons of the past to empower young people who are fighting discrimination today. *Double Charged* was, in its own way, a part of a national before and after given the role the project played in policy change, helping to move juvenile justice approaches from excessive financial punishment to a more humane approach to rehabilitation.

The visual experience of *We Literally Redrew Our Community* provides us with a concrete image through which to see the broader theory of change behind CCE. At this point in our story, we know that the ease of dragging a slider back and forth in no way corresponds to the uneven, messy, challenging, and never-ending work of making that change. Which brings us to one last project. It's perhaps not the most obvious to include in a chapter on coding for joy and hope. The experiences that gave rise to it and the stories it contains were sometimes painful, and there is no triumphant before-and-after outcome that puts that struggle safely in the past. And yet we still see the message behind this project, *In Their Own Words: Beyond the Binary*, as one of joy and hope because of the model that young people set by fighting to make it happen, the healing effect of sharing untold stories with others who relate, and the opportunities the project creates for future young people to find it, resonate with it, and add narratives of their own.

In Their Own Words

In Their Own Words: Beyond the Binary came about under striking circumstances. By 2018, its lead producer, Damian, had written extensively about their nonbinary identity, including several "explainer" essays on pronouns. One piece, called "All Your Questions about Gender Neutral Pronouns Answered," began like this:

> People say the darnedest things about the singular "they."
>
> When I tell someone that my pronouns are they/them/their, I never know what to expect. Sometimes people say okay and move on, but other times, they'll start to ask a whole bunch of questions that I don't really feel like answering. It's usually well intentioned; I get that people are just trying to understand. But I do get tired of explaining the same things over and over.
>
> So to save everyone (myself included) some time and confusion, I've rounded up some responses to the most common weird questions I get about my pronouns.

With humor and patience, Damian goes on to tackle various comments they've encountered, such as "I'm fine with nonbinary people, but I don't believe in singular they pronouns. It makes no sense."[20]

"Not only are you on the wrong side of history, you're also on the wrong side of English, my friend," Damian replies. They cite major dictionaries that have recognized the singular they as grammatically correct for many years. Damian's pronoun stories appeared in *Teen Vogue* and on KQED radio as well as YR Media's own site and social feeds.

The posts were really well received. A collaborator at MIT who is nonbinary even wrote to us to say they had linked to Damian's story in their email signature so that anyone seeing the singular they for the first time could click into Damian's piece to find answers to their questions.

Damian was proud of this work, and as we noted, patient with their readers. But at a certain point, they were ready to move on from the subject of pronouns. There was so much more to say about life as a nonbinary young person than what word they use to refer to themself. There were so many conversations that needed to happen among nonbinary young people beyond explainers for cis readers. So when a major media outlet approached YR to see if Damian would like to create yet another pronoun story, Damian said no. It was a big opportunity to turn down. Yet Damian knew that for them, it was the right thing to do.

Instead, Damian initiated an ambitious project with YR Media's interactive team to create a rich and nuanced multimedia story centering conversations among nonbinary teens and young adults on the themes of coming out, love and dating, race, and presentation.

Like the other projects that we have written about in this chapter, *In Their Own Words* directly addresses the struggles that nonbinary young people face.[21] One contributor describes their heartbreak when they came out as nonbinary and their best friend replied, "Oh, so you're an 'it'?"

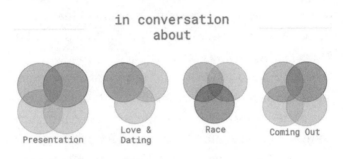

In Their Own Words is an exploration of non-binary gender identity created by non-binary teens and young adults.

in conversation about

Presentation   Love & Dating   Race   Coming Out

Figure 7.4
Screen capture of *In Their Own Words: Beyond the Binary* interactive.

"It's really hard to pin down with words how I move in the world with so many people trying to stick labels on me," writes Julia, "from being told by family while growing up that I had to be masculine, to being told by the kids on the bus that I had 'a little sugar in my bowl,' to being told by racists that dark-skinned Black bodies like mine are masculine by default."

When family members use the words "sister" or "daughter," "I hide my cringing discomfort," writes Rob. While difficult to write and read, these stories of wounds and pain are vital. They ground the project in the real and convey to nonbinary readers that they are not alone.

And yet hope surfaces as well in the conversations featured in *In Their Own Words*. "If I'm wearing makeup and I'm presenting masculine, and someone feels uncomfortable with that," Damian writes, "first, I don't care. And second, part of me is like, 'Good.' You deserve to have those wires crossed for you a little bit because those wires aren't as straight in real life as you think they are." Damian refuses to take on someone else's discomfort. They see it as a lesson that person needs to learn.

"My family loves and supports me," writes Julia. "I used to think they didn't because they would say things that were ignorant. And I don't think they necessarily prepared the world for me as much as they were trying to prepare me for the world." Knowing Julia as we do, and having worked with them on the powerful stories they have gone on to produce after contributing to this one, we know that Julia is out there doing the work of preparing the world for the brilliance and power that exists within themself and their community.

Joy and hope are evident in the fact that these conversations are happening. Damian and their collaborators came together, with and for one another, sharing what is the same and what is different in the arcs of their gender identities. Even the design conveys joy and hope, which are evident in the color scheme, the individual portraits, the audio where you hear qualities in the voices of each author, and the quotes you can share on social media, carrying these vital voices out to wider and wider conversations.

Before *In Their Own Words*, nonbinary young people had fewer places to turn for conversations that reflected their pain and joy. After the project launched, it won an Association of LGBTQ Journalists award, and lay a foundation for deeper, fuller coverage from YR Media's production company centering the experiences of nonbinary and trans youths. As far as what comes next, as with any youth story, it's good to remember that we are all part of deciding what to make of it and where it can take us from here.

8
Tensions and Extensions

Over the course of the prior seven chapters, we have taken you behind the scenes in the making of twelve projects that spanned seven years at YR Media.[1] Combined with the curriculum, pedagogy, and research that informed them, these projects have shaped our CCE framework. Our goal for this book is to share that framework with students, practitioners, program leaders, community advocates, media producers, and scholars within and well beyond STEM fields. If there is one thing we have learned from our experiments with the interactive team over all of these years at YR Media, it's that engaging young people at the intersection of civic engagement, computation, and creative arts has the potential to change the way we approach learning and making across all three of these fields.

It is not just our own work inside YR Media that has given rise to this insight. We are inspired by the programs that we have observed and in some cases participated in with partners who have taken up CCE in their own far-flung learning environments. We thought it a fitting way to close our story by highlighting the ways in which CCE has evolved and expanded across settings, including college-level liberal arts courses, middle and high school CS classes, and museum sites.

We organize this final chapter in two parts. First, we consider some of the tensions that arise within efforts to apply CCE to environments within and beyond places like YR Media. Then we offer three composite "personas," each representing a sector of education where practitioners are using the products and methods of CCE in ways that we hope will inspire further innovation over time. Consider each a kind of personal "point of entry" into the process of imagining where CCE can go from here. Following each persona, we share findings from our real-life collaborators and coconspirators who are taking CCE to the next level by evolving the framework in ways that we could never have conceived of on our own.

Tension #1: Learner-Centered Approaches Put to the Test of Time

When I (Cliff) first arrived at YR Media in spring 2014, I had recently completed my doctoral thesis and was a first-year assistant professor of education. I began my role as YR's scholar-in-residence by sitting in with the interactive team twice a week, audio-recording discussions and taking copious field notes. Still getting used to the community and ethos of YR Media, I began working with individuals and pairs of youth interns, asking them questions about what they were doing, and more important, how they were thinking about their work. "What problem are you trying to fix with the code here [pointing at their screen]? What other troubleshooting techniques have you tried? Why did you use this strategy? How does this connect to the goal of your app? How do you think your users will respond? What messages do you hope your users will learn?" I was a fresh-faced learning scientist, intrigued by the young people's meaning-making processes as they wrestled with their interactive projects. I also routinely checked in with Asha about what I noticed. At one point I suggested that we slow down to ensure that every team member fully comprehended each technical decision and intention behind their work before moving forward. "We only have five weeks left in this session and we have deadlines to meet," Asha noted, seeming a bit skeptical, and immediately I felt a sense of déjà vu. Three years earlier, I had been coteaching and collecting data for my dissertation in a Los Angeles high school CS classroom. I recalled the same pressures that Asha was managing—in my case due to the constraints of school bell schedules, semester marking periods, and my own internal deadlines. I chuckled knowingly and said to Asha, "My bad. You're right."

This example during my first months at YR Media underscores the tension between time-intensive deep learning and the realities of school schedules, arbitrary marking periods, and the ten-week session lengths and deadlines of our media company. Even work in an out-of-school context does not operate with unlimited time, resources, and personnel. While we have more flexibility than a lot of classroom teachers, most of our projects have clear deadlines and require coordinating with multiple individuals from various departments, such as journalism, design, video, music, communications, and so on. Sometimes we're producing interactive projects with outside media partners, and we typically need to account for grant deadlines and parameters as well.

Tensions like these grow exponentially within a school context. I remember the challenges of teaching fifty-minute periods and spending the first ten cajoling thirty-five teens wandering in from lunch, getting them situated, and attempting to rearrange them back into their respective project groups. On any given day, group members may be absent, late, or checked out. So realistically, how much work time and in-depth discussion can you squeeze in to talk about the technical nuances of their project as it relates to disrupting systems that cause harm?

Even at YR Media, where interns are paid employees and youth-to-adult ratios usually hover below a dreamy ten to one, we still deal with the demanding schedules of high schoolers juggling multiple responsibilities, like jobs, childcare for siblings, sports, school events, activities, projects, SAT/ACT prep classes, family obligations, and cultural and spiritual participation, all the while maintaining their academic work as full-time students.

If you've had the opportunity to experience YR Media interactives, you likely have sensed how labor intensive each one was to build. From researching, ideation, design, and coding, to troubleshooting, editing, testing, and retesting, each one took months, if not years, to complete. Nearly two years went by between the initial *West Side Stories* brainstorm you witnessed in the opening paragraphs of this book and the final launch. Numerous team members floated in and out of the project. An undertaking of this magnitude would be challenging to replicate in a classroom context, to say the least.

That said, we have seen youth participatory action research colleagues in after-school settings, with a dedicated team of teen and adult collaborators, create incredible social impact projects through yearlong investigations and presentations about unfair, oppressive schooling practices.[2] What if their youth participatory action research team had access to young people with the technical and critical knowledge to build an interactive that complemented their social actions? We have observed robust collaborations between school-based robotics teams and industry experts who lent their time, resources, and know-how to support youth learning and product development. Rather than frame these partnerships as charitable opportunities for adults and their corporate affiliations, what if these "professional" collaborators learned to challenge the taken-for-granted goals, missions, and everyday practices of their companies? Our YR Media counterstories can serve as the motivation and foundation for the development of humane apps for good. Opportunities for young people and adults to develop critical, computational, creative products are mutually beneficial for both parties.

Tension #2: Diverse Learner Experiences, Backgrounds, and Attitudes

At YR Media, teens enrolled in AP CS classes sit side by side with peers who chose the interactive department because they liked the instructor or had a friend who had signed up. Many youth interns on the team have never coded a day in their lives. Some of these same young people have expressed apprehensions, insecurities, and negative associations with computer programming and technology, particularly the ways in which these fields have produced hostile environments for their racial, gender, and class communities. These concerns don't just evaporate once they join the interactive team. What's more, new interns arrive on the first day of each new YR session seated next to peers who have been in the department for multiple sessions. While the dynamics of such a diverse community of practice create undeniable challenges for teachers and learners alike, we see this same dimension of our environment as part of our edge.

While youth creators with prior experience know more about coding than interns who are trying it out for the first time, it becomes clear that the "old heads" have not exhausted their learning potential when they are tasked with ideating and creating wireframes on topics important to them with each new session. Likewise, novices bring fresh perspectives to partially completed prior projects where seasoned interns have gotten stuck. Compared to a purely skills-driven model, our process-oriented approach allows for multiple points of entry for youth learners. At various junctures each session, we split up the group to lead targeted workshops for those with limited coding experience. This, too, can be a great opportunity for peer teaching; more expert interns strengthen their knowledge by teaching others what they have recently learned.

Tension #3: Collaborative Practice versus Individual Skill

In all interactive team sessions, individual students have opportunities to develop their personal coding, design, and data skills by building out a specific part of a collaborative project. But our overarching goal is for everyone to contribute to the shared outcome of a strong finished product, and that means that especially for interns who only stay with us for one or two sessions, their individual competencies might reach greater breadth than depth; they learn a little bit of everything. Those who reapply to our department for multiple sessions across several projects have more of an opportunity to develop solo expertise in a specific area, like ideation, design, algorithmic problem-solving, data analysis, coding, optimization, user and market research, and so on. That said, even for young people who persist over months or years, transitioning to learning environments governed by individual performance and testing represents a significant, sometimes jarring shift.

In the past, we have experimented with badges to certify that young people have achieved specific skills. Some students loved the idea that they could accumulate badges through their time at YR Media, marking their progress. Others were turned off by this solo skills-oriented approach. It struck them as too much like school and incompatible with the collaborative environment that they had come to appreciate at a place like YR. Part of the motivation for many of our YR Media creators is the opportunity to develop relationships with other young people from different walks of life, and tap into our collective experiences to build distinctive critical, computational, and creative approaches to thinking and acting in the world. They were concerned that individual certifications couldn't begin to capture that shared dynamic. We continue to explore ways to implement certifications that recognize individual accomplishments while honoring joint effort and understanding.

Consistent with YR Media's model of collegial pedagogy, young people don't "code alone." Experienced professional developers, designers, and engineers work in tandem with youth creators in every phase of each project. The polished computational products we have shared throughout these pages represent an intergenerational team effort. Adult staff members will rework, finish, or clean up code, edit and fact-check copy, contribute to and refine design elements, and question or challenge the direction of a project at any point. To expect novice teen creators to produce and publish interactives like the ones we describe here, on their own, in the span of a school semester, wouldn't make sense. Yet with the right support, more time, a shift in pedagogical approach, and guided access to existing open-source software and templates, we think it is possible.

Partnerships with media and tech organizations, alumni, or even a local college's CS department can create opportunities to turn ideas and wireframes into functioning interactives and apps. In chapter 2, we referenced one such collaboration in the form of the land acknowledgment SMS and Facebook Messenger bot from the nonprofit Native Land. This partnership between an Indigenous-led organization and local coders appears to be a model for cross-sector, mission-driven work that, in this case, condemns settler colonialism while countering the erasure of native communities by the governments of Canada, the United States, and other countries around the world.[3] This project and others demonstrate the possibilities of a CCE framework that values community expertise as a crucial driver of tech-enabled social change.

Finding the "right" balance between engaging deep youth learning and publishing audience-ready products is a challenge that we have not fully resolved, nor do we ever expect to. More important than devising the perfect formula is acknowledging this reality, creating collegial checks and balances, and always seeking ways to broaden youth leadership and learning, all the while distributing opportunities equitably, and in ways that build the strengths of team members and prepare them to meet deadlines with excellence. We want to demystify, analyze, critique, and remake the technologies ubiquitous in our lives, while partnering with young people to learn the skills and sustain the practices to challenge others to do the same. We aim for young people systemically and historically underserved and frequently marginalized in CS and other fields to see themselves along with their communities in the tools and platforms that they make, modify, and reimagine, at YR Media and beyond.

And beyond is where we turn next—via a set of personas based on real-life innovators who have found ways to enact CCE in a range of learning environments, establishing justice-driven approaches to teach and make at the intersection of computation and media arts.

Persona #1: Humanities Professor

You are a history professor in a college of liberal arts at a large, public university. You have affiliations across a number of departments: sociology, education, ethnic studies, and English. You have taught topics as wide-ranging as the prison-industrial complex, the foundations of educational inequality, housing displacement and gentrification, cultural hegemony, settler colonialism, and critical examinations of authorial voice and its legitimacy. You and your colleagues have often struggled to engage undergraduates in completing reading assignments. Since the global pandemic beginning in 2020, this challenge has grown dramatically more difficult. The same two to three students tend to dominate class discussions. Despite your best efforts to bring in guest speakers, introduce new journal articles and texts, and utilize diverse discussion formats, most students seem resigned to turning in essays that reflect little passion or personal connections with the material. Many students simply repeat the concepts from readings without much critical analysis or application to real-world issues.

The opportunity: to diversify the texts that you feature in your classes to deepen student engagement and spark their deep thinking about fundamental questions like, What is history? Whose stories count? How do we make meaning from artifacts? On whose land do we live?

Voices from the Fields of Social Science and Humanities

Expanding Authorship through Nonlinear, Multimodal Texts

Mario Hernandez is a sociology professor at a small women's college. In a course titled Sociology of Oakland, he and his students analyze changes over the course of that city's history. To prepare students to engage in discussions related to the power of media in shaping narratives, he juxtaposes two texts. The first is a highly sensationalized 2009 cable television show, *Gang Wars: Oakland*. The second, an Emmy award-winning 1981 PBS documentary called *Children of Violence*, depicts the lives and deaths of Latino teenagers who belong to gangs. Hernandez places these two videos ahead of his introduction to YR Media's *West Sides Stories* to contrast those mainstream media portrayals with an Oakland narrative where young people directed the storytelling.

Hernandez's approach picks up a refrain in the humanities: Who has the authority and legitimacy to shape a community's story? All three texts that Hernandez uses explore the lived realities of people who struggle to sustain themselves and their communities without the basic material means to survive. The gaudy one-dimensional depictions of wild teens in *Gang Wars: Oakland* left his students skeptical and frustrated. While they appreciated the more nuanced perspective on poverty offered by *Children of Violence*, Hernandez's students questioned some of the editorial decisions of its director, an outsider to Oakland. By the time they got to *West Side Stories*, students were struck by the various ways it stood apart from the other two texts. The project sparked feelings of introspection, intrigue, and inspiration.

"I try to bring up, 'Who's writing this history?'" Hernandez told us. The YR Media producers "aren't even, quote-unquote, historians," he said. "Except that they are, in the sense that, 'Who gets to be the historian?' That is the question that I think is always lingering in my work. . . . What counts as history? And how do we empower people to tell their story?"

When his students think of history, they imagine "big history, big events, big actors," Hernandez has noticed. *West Side Stories* shows them that "everyday history is important . . . the power of people's everyday experiences." Students in Hernandez's class were moved by the voices of actual residents discussing their experiences with gentrification. "It makes a huge difference to me as to who gets to tell stories," said one student. "This was a breath of fresh air, that BIPOC teens and young adults are telling the story about Oakland." "I was very excited about the youth empowerment on display," her classmate added. "I asked my nine-year-old daughter to come look at several of the projects. There is so much power in the youth voice, and it needs to be reinforced and encouraged."

The project's nonlinear, multimodal storytelling format stood out from the course's other assigned materials. Hernandez noted the "different, simultaneous narratives, where [users] can bounce around. . . . You can engage with different sensory perspectives." Unlike a static, linear text, *West Side Stories* allows users to choose the order in which they hear voices, see videos, read copy, and circumnavigate the map. In real life, multiple events unfold simultaneously, and the project's design matches that experience. With phones, laptops, and various types of media at his students' fingertips at all times, Hernandez constantly competes for their attention—more so than ever under the remote learning conditions of the COVID-19 pandemic. Rather than resent those devices as sources of distraction, Hernandez used them to introduce digital media stories that engaged students where and how they already consume content.

One student in particular, a twenty-year-old undergraduate, opens a window into the difference that projects like *West Side Stories* can make for learners. She lives in West Oakland and passes a mural featured in *West Side Stories* everyday. Now, using the map, she has learned the story behind it. "Young, BIPOC teens and youth are coming up with these important topics, and then transforming them into interactive, interesting, and creative projects. I think projects like the ones at YR Media engrave confidence in these young people and give them something to be passionate about, which a lot of formal education forgets to incorporate into their standard curriculum."

This student hopes to become a teacher. *West Side Stories* inspired her to learn more about the media and the role it could play in her future classroom. As a recent high school graduate, she knows all too well that traditional, standards-based education rarely offers projects that are passion driven, interdisciplinary, and community responsive. She envisions the sense of empowerment that projects combining computational thinking with social analysis and creative expression can instill in students and young adults like her. "I took coding last semester and liked it more than I thought I would. It's exciting to see projects . . . that are [not simply] using tech to make mindless games or apps, but are thinking about ways technology can actually make change within communities." Rather than just churn out code, she sees the potential to use computational thinking and other technical know-how to address structural problems, and re-reinvent, remix, and reimagine personal expression and community life.

By the time we spoke with Hernandez, there was only about a month left in a semester that took place entirely online. He couldn't tell us what this student looked or sounded like, because she had never turned on her camera or spoken up in class discussions. *West Side Stories* broke through that thick, pandemic-era "Zoom fatigue." Imagine what's possible under conditions more favorable to student engagement.

Reclaiming Place through a Critical Examination of Maps

What happens when you take the *West Side Stories* project even further afield—to a different discipline, in a different country? Robyn Ilten-Gee is an assistant professor of teacher education at Simon Fraser University in British Columbia, Canada. Prior to graduate school, she worked as a producer in YR Media's newsroom and so it came naturally to Ilten-Gee to draw from the organization's archive when she planned her college-level courses. She

used *West Side Stories* with a cohort of preservice teachers to demonstrate how young people combined coding and storytelling to reclaim place as well as combat
"land amnesia." Using a social justice and decolonizing
lens, Ilten-Gee prepares new teachers by asking "what it
means to practice education on land that was colonized
by white settlers and how Indigenous perspectives can
inform practice." She implored her students to think
critically about maps: "Who decides what landmarks are
denoted, which boundaries are drawn, and what streets/
parks are named?" Like Hernandez, Ilten-Gee used *West
Side Stories* to reveal "how young people are creating
counternarratives of place, flipping the script on stereotypes about their own communities, and telling stories
that 'settlers' or gentrifiers may not ever uncover."

For many aspiring teachers, a critical first step in developing a sense of intellectual and cultural humility is to
accept that we all wear blinders as a result of our own col-
onizing schooling experiences, and our continual social-
ization into white supremacy, patriarchy, and capitalism.
Many of us have to keep unlearning state-sanctioned
ideologies, historical narratives, and ways of knowing
that privilege those in power. With *West Side Stories*, Ilten-
Gee's students interrogated taken-for-granted features on
maps, such as landmarks, boundaries, and the names of
streets and parks. They grappled with the roots of their
worldviews, uncovering new pathways for intellectual
development. Unlike the United States, Canada has at
least begun to take public responsibility for its genocidal

treatment of Indigenous people by mandating localized First Nations curriculum in some schools.[4] By historicizing the land, Ilten-Gee formed an approach to teacher education that centers Indigenous perspectives. Paradoxically, she recognized that a digital product that reflects present and future computational power can play a key role in reestablishing teachers' consciousness of history and inherited orientations toward place.

Mood Ring as a Model for Social-Emotional Learning

Ilten-Gee has integrated *Mood Ring* into her teaching too—in this case, in a graduate education course on children's social development. She paired the app with readings on the impacts of technology on young peoples' lives. "Youth-produced apps like *Mood Ring* not only provide practical solutions for supporting emotional and mental well-being," Ilten-Gee has found. They can also reveal how "the act of creating the app/coding can actually be an act of agency that contributes to social-emotional health."[5] Her research on critical digital literacy explores "how young people's interactions with media can facilitate critical reasoning processes, particularly about issues of fairness, harm, rights, social norms, and personal preference." Her scholarship has found that youth-produced media artifacts "demonstrate complicated and nuanced moral-social reasoning about history, representation, and justice." By engaging in coding for accountability and creating counternarratives that challenge stereotypes of young people, the creators

"wrestle with multiple concerns and arrive at complicated conclusions about their world and their life."

Unbeknownst to Ilten-Gee, the research that the
creators of *Mood Ring* carried out in developing their
concept for the app did exactly what she described. As
we've discussed, the team consulted with Stefan Goldstone, a YR Media staff member and longtime psychiatric social worker and mental health provider.

"The YR participants were way ahead of where I was,"
Goldstone said. "[They] had already thought through
a lot of the key questions—and the potential pitfalls,
such as an app that leads people toward self-diagnosis
(diagnosis should always be done by a clinically trained
mental health / behavioral health professional), or an
app that causes alarm or anxiety when aggregating symp-
toms over a stretch of time." Through their research,
the youth creators came together with a subject matter
expert to explore the ethics of mental health, youth privacy and protections, cost-benefit analyses of the app's
features, and social norms and stigmas. These are rich
conversations whose implications extend beyond any
one CCE project.

Revisiting Our Humanities Professors

What Hernandez and Ilten-Gee have illustrated here is
the ability to reach their students in new ways with the
content and process of CCE. They used YR Media content
to contextualize, complement, and challenge the authority of other assigned texts. The interactives reflect young

people's capacity to contend with challenging social dilemmas while developing the expertise to tell their stories and create computational products for change. Elevating youth-made interactives into the college classroom challenges traditional notions of knowledge. What counts? How can we move beyond linear texts? By broadening course content into multimodal products, educators reflect where and how most of us receive information today, and show students that academic experts and peer-reviewed publications are not the sole purveyors of wisdom. They cultivate in students the agency to become intellectuals and knowledge creators in their own right.

Our examples so far have centered on higher education. When young people combine code, critique, and creative expression, their products have a great deal to offer secondary classroom contexts as well. Imagine for a minute how an eleventh grader in a US history class might engage with *West Side Stories* in a civil rights unit, especially once they realize that teens and young adults created the project. Instead of only reading about nine teenagers who desegregated Central High School in 1957, what if students today explored the multimedia content from YR Media's *LR9LIVE* project and shared their thoughts on Twitter for homework? A teacher could follow up by having students create their own social media-based reenactment of a historic event, interviewing family members and peers, investigating local or online archives, and even imagining interactions with figures who were on the ground at the time. These activities personalize and build connections between young people's present-day lives and themes across history, at the same time that they connect critical social analysis with technology and art.

With the growth of social and emotional learning in K–12 schools, English language arts teachers could use the *Mood Ring* app to build habits of mindfulness and self-awareness. Students could begin by using *Mood Ring* to track their feelings and thoughts for two weeks, noticing patterns that emerge over time. They could then look at the work of various spoken word performers, identifying how those artists convey emotions using words and other modes of expression. Students could create their own poems, monologues, dialogues, short stories, or vignettes related to what they discovered about themselves. These activities align with English language arts standards for reading and writing texts that call on students to examine "the meaning of words and phrases as they are used in the text, including figurative and connotative meanings; analyze the cumulative impact of specific word choices on meaning and tone. . . . Use narrative techniques, such as dialogue, pacing, description, reflection, and multiple plot lines, to develop experiences, events, and/or characters. . . . Use precise words and phrases, telling details, and sensory language to convey a vivid picture of the experiences, events, setting, and/or characters."[6] Following YR Media tradition, teachers could create opportunities for students to publish their products for audiences within and beyond the school, building further engagement and authenticity into the learning experience.

Persona #2: CS Department Head

You lead the CS department of a large urban school district. As a result of your team's strategic negotiations and dedication, your district now offers introductory and AP CS courses across all of your secondary schools. Your team of teachers, however, is troubled to find an enrollment gap and poor retention rates for female, Black, and Latinx students. Sadly, this pattern mirrors national CS education trends at the secondary and collegiate levels. As a passionate technology equity advocate, you are looking for ideas to change this outcome.

The opportunity: to transform and diversify participation in CS pathways by basing projects on youth-produced stories from communities that have been systemically marginalized, and connecting technical skills to sociopolitical realities and creative imagination.

Voices from the Field of CS

The Power of Stories in App Development
Selim Tezel heads up the App Inventor Education team at MIT's Computer Science and Artificial Intelligence Laboratory. With the leadership of MIT professor Hal

Abelson, Tezel and his colleagues have partnered with YR Media for more than a decade to enhance their App Inventor system, and create curriculum that deepens and democratizes CS education. The MIT team focuses primarily on middle and high school–aged youths with limited prior experience in CS. Tezel and his colleagues work with YR Media to ground app development in storytelling.

Tezel learned to appreciate the power of narrative in the realm of technology from the late MIT professor Patrick Winston, a leader in AI. Winston "spent much time thinking about what makes human intelligence so different from the intelligence of primates," Tezel told us. "He identified our capacity to tell, understand, recombine, and share stories as the most significant characteristic that distinguishes our human intelligence." For Tezel, YR Media stories "always give us pause, and ground us in real and complex aspects of the human condition. They provide us with wonderful societal context, help establish a human connection, and ultimately inspire us with a deep sense of empathy for the communities we serve."

Leveraging the values that Tezel describes, YR Media and MIT App Inventor launched an initiative, *Youth Mobile Power*, to support young people building humane technology.[7] For each segment in the series, YR Media youth reporters produce a story, and share it with Tezel and his team. Our MIT partners then build the starter code for a mobile app with tutorials that guide users to create their own apps inspired by YR Media's reporting. The series has been accessed by well over a hundred thousand users across the world.

In one YR Media story featured in *Youth Mobile Power*, the author describes growing up as a bilingual Spanish-English speaker who translated for her mother at school, doctors' offices, and other English-only places. The writer went from resenting those responsibilities to appreciating all that her mom has gone through, navigating environments where she has had to struggle to be understood. Based on this story, Tezel's team created a tutorial that young people could use to develop a "translation app" that aids immigrant parents who find themselves in English-speaking situations.[8] "Building this code is so simple," Tezel said. "And that really gives kids, I think, a sense of empowerment. . . . As human beings, we are meaning-seeking creatures. If we have meaning, we are motivated, we are interested. We work harder."[9]

Youth Mobile Power also includes a tutorial based on a pair of YR Media stories related to mental health. "Only Smiling on the Outside" is the story of two teens who rely on each other as they cope with post-traumatic depression.[10] In "Could Your Next Therapist Be Your Phone?," teens and experts weigh the pros and cons of AI technology in therapeutic contexts.[11] Linking also to the *Mood Ring* app, this tutorial walks App Inventor users through the steps of developing their own mobile tool to support young people's resilience and well-being.

This installment in the *Youth Mobile Power* series prompts young people to consider what it takes to develop computational products that are sensitive to multilayered, unquantifiable, difficult-to-predict human behaviors. The project prompts youth developers to explore the

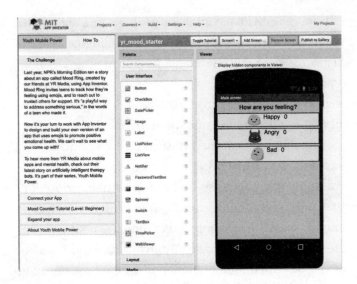

Figure 8.1
Screen capture of MIT App Inventor's *Youth Mobile Power* series.

ethical and existential implications of their work: "Can you ever endow a machine to feel empathy or even emulate empathy? Will machine intelligence ever come close to human intelligence? How do you teach [empathy] to a machine?" These questions align with what Tezel's MIT colleagues Michael Tissenbaum, Josh Sheldon, and Hal Abelson call "computational action," which nurtures computational identity and digital empowerment by creating products that have a real impact on the lives of the developers and their communities.[12] With computational action, the next generation of mobile app developers creates digital tools that lead with our shared capacity for compassion and mutual aid.

Cultural Context Matters

While conscious of the dystopian dimensions of our technological future, Tezel and his team sought to make fun and engaging curriculum materials for CS teachers and their students. They were able to do so while adhering to the Computer Science Teachers of America K–12 CS Standards, as evident in two tutorials they created as companions to YR Media's *Erase Your Face* and *Can You Teach AI to Dance?*

Leveraging the popularity of Instagram's facial filters to spark youth engagement, the MIT team created the *Facemesh Filter Camera* to introduce young people to the role of facial landmark detection in machine learning. The tutorial starts by inviting users to play with YR Media's *Erase Your Face*, which, as you might recall, was our interactive that challenges users to explore how much obscuring is necessary to dodge detection by facial recognition systems. Users of the tutorial learn how the technology works and then get to create their own custom filters with MIT App Inventor.[13]

Figure 8.2
Screen capture of the Computer Science and Artificial Intelligence Laboratory's *Facemesh Filter Camera.*

While this tutorial in itself was a powerful extension of YR Media's original story, Tezel told us about a long-time collaborator with the MIT team, retired CS professor Fujio Yamamoto, who went one step further. Yamamoto redesigned the *Facemesh Filter Camera* for a Japanese cultural context, updating the algorithm to recognize facial gestures and movements that are specific to Japanese communicative practices.[14] He documented his process through a blog post where he questions, extends, and enhances the MIT App Inventor tools.[15]

Yamamoto's update reminds us that when designers tune into human variation and recognize how their own positionality imprints on their products, they develop more powerful tools to engage and serve diverse communities, including those unseen and ill served by technology. As Ruja Benjamin argues in her book *Race after Technology*, viewing technology as an apolitical tool of efficiency masks the subtle and overt beliefs, biases, and human tendencies that shape its design and impact.[16] Joy Buolamwini and Timnit Gebru's groundbreaking studies of racial and gender bias in facial recognition systems in particular lay bare these biases, and contextualize even MIT App Inventor's playful facial filter experiments in the dead-serious context of discrimination as a force that can both shape and be a product of AI.[17]

Imagine if more of our CS classes created space for students to openly discuss, analyze, critique, update, or entirely reinvent tools based on their insights and lived experiences as BIPOC, immigrant, or trans youths. What would they make? What lively discussions might they have? A teacher could invite students to brainstorm and re-create an AI tool like facial recognition software so that it is culturally responsive to all the students in the class. They could begin by asking, How does this algorithm work? What variables does it use to make predictions? What variables or data points are missing? How can this tool disrupt the linked phenomena of white supremacy, wealth inequality, mass surveillance, and cultural erasure?

Expression and Humanity by the Numbers?

You may remember *Can You Teach AI to Dance?* from our chapter on coding for creative expression. This is the project that interrogated AI by inviting users to rate the danceability of songs on a Spotify playlist and then compare their personal judgments with the scores that Spotify used machine learning to determine. Tezel and his team tried to design a tutorial that would allow users to re-create *Can You Teach AI to Dance?* functionality with App Inventor, but they hit a snag. Spotify's licensing terms prohibited the display of danceability scores, in real time, based on users' song preferences. So the App Inventor team had to pivot, and go back into research and ideation mode.

The App Inventor team members realized that while YR Media focused on the relationship between AI and music, their tutorial could explore related themes, but this time through dance. In their research, Tezel and his colleagues came across a tool called PoseNet, "a machine learning model that allows for real-time human pose estimation."[18] It uses computer vision to detect human figures in videos and recognize specific poses. The tool can be used to test how well a user matches a real-life pose to one they see on the screen.

Tezel and his team had the idea to use PoseNet to create a data set of iconic dance moves, like John Travolta's indelible disco pose in the film *Saturday Night Fever*: one finger pointed in the air, one toward the ground, one arm raised, legs spread apart, and hips to one side. Users could emulate each pose and score points based on how well they hit the move. Tezel admits that this user experience doesn't come anywhere near capturing the beauty of dance. Still, it pushed him and his team to ponder profound questions like, Can we come up with a quantifiable system that represents ineffable dance aesthetics? "And in most cases, I don't think there's an answer," Tezel admitted. "It's a mystery at the end of the day. But that doesn't mean you can't have fun with it."

The *Awesome Dancing with AI Tutorial* that our MIT partners developed out of these explorations aimed to spark fun for users and get them to grapple with some of the same questions the design team contemplated as it produced the tutorial: "whether something as organic and complex as a dance can be quantified, measured, and mathematically studied with the help of AI."

The project operates in the spaces between human and machine, aesthetics and mathematical measurement,

Figure 8.3
Screen capture of the Computer Science and Artificial Intelligence
Laboratory's *Awesome Dancing with AI Tutorial*.

expression and mechanics, not as mutually exclusive
concepts in opposition, but as intersecting realms. As
young people move through the steps of the tutorial,
they connect computational thinking to disciplines as
wide-ranging as philosophy, anthropology, sociology,
and the performance arts. This is CCE in action.

Revisiting the persona of our CS department head who struggles with the enrollment and retention of underrepresented students, consider for a moment what it might look like to adopt some of the same curricular and pedagogical strategies that Tezel and his team used to make their tutorials. *Facemesh Filter Camera* and *Awesome Dancing with AI Tutorial* cultivate curiosity and joy. Imagine if an introductory CS class began with these two tutorials. How many tenth graders or first-year college students would consider taking additional CS classes if their orientation to the field startled them into an awareness of the profound ways that the software operating on their phones engineers cultural and creative practices, like music and dance, that shape how they literally as well as figuratively move through the world? They could question the feasibility and purpose of using computational tools and algorithms to represent artistic forms and creative expressions, much like Tezel and his team. A teacher could add ethical dimensions to these lessons by introducing the history of racial bias and normalized beauty standards perpetuated by social media filters and algorithms.[19] We have found that when young people get to build tools and tell stories that probe questions they care deeply about at the intersection of technology and creativity, their belief in those products, and their motivation to get them into the hands of users and audiences, sustains them through the hard work of acquiring the necessary skills to turn their visions into reality.

Persona #3: Art and Science Museum Program Director

As a museum program director in an urban city center, you were hired to bring in fresh approaches to connect with local, underserved communities. While seen as an important cultural and educational institution, your museum has developed a reputation for being elitist and old-school. Since your arrival, you have brought in new programs, exhibits, installations, and workshops that have been well received by elementary school–aged children and their teachers on field trips. The Friday night happy hour events keep growing in popularity among young professionals. A key demographic that is still sorely absent, however, are teens and twentysomethings, particularly BIPOC youths and those who see the museum as prohibitively expensive as well as out of step with their cultural touchstones and interests.

The opportunity: to connect with and give voice to traditionally underserved museumgoers using transmedia projects designed and developed by young people.

Voices from the Field of Museums and Cultural Institutions

From Digital to Physical: Interactives in Place
Founded in 1969, the Oakland Museum of California (OMCA) sits on the edge of Lake Merritt, Chinatown, and downtown. Its programming spans art, history, and

the natural sciences. The OMCA takes pride in its inclusiveness. Recent exhibits include Queer California; Black Power; Respect: Hip-Hop Style and Wisdom; and annual programs for Dia de los Muertos, the Lunar New Year, and Juneteenth.[20] So it didn't come as a surprise when the OMCA approached YR Media about transforming *West Side Stories*, our digital map of gentrifying West Oakland, into a physical exhibit. The installation became part of Oakland, I Want You to Know . . . , a collection of exhibits that encouraged attendees to examine the "accelerating social, economic, and demographic change in West Oakland through the wide-ranging perspectives of folks in the community."[21]

To create this program, artist Chris Treggiari and OMCA curator of public practice Evelyn Orantes solicited insights from neighborhood elders, business owners, young people, and even recent transplants attempting to build community through urban farms. The exhibition leaders started with a few key questions: What does home mean to you? Who has the right to space? How is the land used? How should it be used? They utilized video and audio installations, images, and book-making projects to showcase the voices and sentiments of Oakland's diverse communities. The physical space was "inspired by iconic West Oakland buildings—a classic Victorian home, a contemporary loft, a community garden, and the now-shuttered historic Esther's Orbit Room."[22]

The *West Side Stories* exhibit was set up to look like the interior of a BART train, complete with handholds, lights, and a physical version of our digital map where the subway map would normally appear. Pay phone receivers were installed so that participants could listen to audio excerpts from the digital version of our interactive map (see figure 8.4).

One visitor to the OMCA installation was impressed that it "wasn't trying to memorialize Oakland as if this battle has already been lost and we're looking back at it nostalgically. [The exhibition] is looking toward the past but also toward the present."

Her companion concurred:

> The curators of the media content did a good job of getting really authentic and important sound-bites from people who are within the community, whether they're on the side of being a victim, or they're trying to go against the system and [find] local solutions to some of these challenges [in] their community. . . . I thought that was pretty incredible. I also love the ode to Pullman Porters and Black Panthers and just all the historical significance of West Oakland, and the music.

It's striking how closely these themes and takeaways correspond to the aspirations that Kendrick and Yonas expressed in their earliest brainstorms for what became *West Side Stories*. Visitors left with a greater understanding of Oakland's history and important questions interrogating their role in the changing city going forward. The museum environment created a different experience than the one that YR Media could produce on its own. Rather than experience *West Side Stories* alone on

Figure 8.4
Picture of OMCA's re-creation of our *West Side Stories* interactive in a
BART train installation.

their screens, visitors to the OCMA version of the project stepped into a physical space with others, encountering its varied voices, images, and narratives in an embodied, tactile way. A review of the exhibit framed the experience as a social practice, noting how the work crossed disciplinary boundaries and formats: "Social practice projects might look like just about anything—journalism, community organizing, even a shop. The goal is to create social change by staging actions that engage people and make them think—and talk."[23]

What Treggiari and Orantes created here should serve notice to museum staffers who struggle with engaging new visitors, particularly younger, BIPOC, and other underserved museum patrons. By inviting community members to share their stories in the ways they want to be represented, museums flip the script of whose voice matters, and whose artistry is worthy of collection and display not as artifacts frozen in time but instead in the context of a community's dynamic creativity. While the OCMA exhibit offers fresh ways for museums to orient themselves in relation to community, it also contains a provocation for those of us whose comfort zone is to publish products for digital release alone. When we reimagine coded projects in ways that transcend devices and even screens—when we come up with ways for these same products to take shape through physical materials in collective spaces where our communities gather in person—we have the potential to find new audiences, modes of engagement, and avenues to impact for our work.

CCE for Teen Engagement

Halfway around the world is a different museum gallery, where a few teens huddle somewhat awkwardly around a monitor, and debate and rate the danceability of various pop songs playing on the screen. It's Friday night, and a young woman is cajoling the teens to join her on the floor to play out their ratings in real life—in other words, to actually dance. The young woman is a youth adviser for Science Gallery Dublin. The twenty or so teenagers milling around the gallery have recently completed the museum's weeklong program on the topic of AI. They explored coding, electronics, and robotics. This evening's social event takes place among various interactive exhibits that the museum put together to show the young people how the themes they looked at over the course of the week can manifest in art. As you may have figured out, one of the pieces on display was YR Media's *Can You Teach AI to Dance?*

Mairéad Hurley was Science Gallery Dublin's head of research and learning at the time. She created educational programs for the museum's teen and young adult participants. Unlike traditional museums, Science Gallery Dublin has no permanent collection. Instead it houses a series of three to four temporary exhibitions per year.[24] What began in 2008 as a stand-alone learning space at Trinity College in Ireland has expanded to a network of nine galleries around the world. Its goal is to bring "science, art, technology and design together to deliver world-class educational and cultural experiences for young people."[25]

The After Hours event that featured a live version of *Can You Teach AI to Dance?* was part of the European ARTificial Intelligence Lab, a collaborative project between thirteen cultural centers around Europe that sought to bring "AI related scientific and technological topics to general citizens and art audiences in order to contribute to a critical and reflective society."[26] After Hours exhibits invited teens to examine virtual reality, biomedical engineering, and electronics; screen AI-generated movies; and of course, dance to songs while learning about AI.[27] These events were designed for the fifteen- to eighteen-year-old set. Much of the Science Gallery Dublin programming for teens and young adults was "very structured and tied to school attendance," Hurley had noticed. She wanted to create more options that were genuinely driven by the interests of teens. The event brought in nearly two hundred visitors.

Outside Science Gallery Dublin's regular open hours and special events are five-day immersive arts and science workshops. Staff members work with youth advisers to develop curriculum and pedagogy linked thematically to current or upcoming exhibitions. In the workshop series on AI and robotics, for example, participants learned circuit building, created a diorama with embedded electronics based on an Irish folktale, and participated in a "take a stand" activity, where they moved around the gallery space and debated an ethical issue in AI. The gallery's pedagogical strategies are as wide-ranging as their topics, but they all connect back to AI's influence in the arts, culture, religion, and other domains of Irish life. The twenty teens began to build connections with one another over the course of the week, according to Hurley, and she observed this sense of community at the After Hours event, where youth program participants were the ones leading conversations at the various installations.

"They had ownership of the space," Hurley said. "You can't just flip a switch and make young people talk to you about the things that you think are the right things." One way that Science Gallery Dublin builds that sense of ownership is by engaging young adults as mediators in their exhibit spaces. Before they take on those roles, the young people receive training in the communication and facilitation of science and arts learning so that they are prepared to draw the public into a dialogue about the museum's exhibits. "I definitely think it helps younger audiences engage with the work more because they kind of come in and they see someone like them who comes up and wants to talk to them," said Hurley. It helps that curators seek out work that engages all the senses—"things you can touch, things you can play with, taste, or smell."

Imagine what a difference it makes if, on entering a museum, instead of encountering a solemn, hushed hall with images and artifacts behind glass, you find a colorful, boisterous atmosphere with young people engaging you in conversation and activities related to the work on display. Rather than simply learning about an established artist's or scientist's process, the young adult mediator puts you in the position of creator, imagining how you might approach a similar project. As sociocultural researchers, we have long known the power of learners making meaning through discourse with more expert others, and by utilizing tools and materials in their environments versus considering abstract concepts alone.[28] Youth mediators at Science Gallery Dublin develop a specific kind of expertise that enables them to collapse the artificial distance between formal science and art knowledge, community relevance, and youth engagement. They learn to ask pointed questions, offer just-in-time information and resources, and build on the background experiences of visitors. They provide an opportunity for patrons to make their own meaning of exhibited work, meeting them where they are.

Employing young people as dialogic facilitators for peers and the public is a powerful pedagogical model that should be common practice in any exhibition space seeking to broaden its appeal to teens and young adults.[29] When the work on display combines technology and creative expression through an ethics lens, peer facilitators are especially well positioned to help visitors make connections across these three domains, and see how cultural products that integrate science and art relate to themes that shape our communities and the human condition. "Museums and galleries are social spaces that can be part of their cultural life . . . and social life," Hurley said. About teens and young adults, Hurley added, "The programs are for them, the exhibitions are for them." Who better than young people themselves, then, to engage the public in what museums have to offer, and to translate coded products like *Can You Teach AI to Dance?* into collective, embodied, place-based learning experiences?

In Summary

Through our three personas, we have seen what's possible when adults and young people come together to design ecosystems that challenge traditional approaches to teaching and model transdisciplinary ways of learning. What emerges is not simply a mix of different disciplines but rather a type of xenogenesis, where the outcome is something new. This is the outcome we seek through the CCE framework. The ultimate idea is not for young people to toggle between science, civics, and art but instead for them to dwell in the dynamic spaces in between, to discover that novel insight, technique, or crucial question that will sustain their engagement as they design digital products that transcend screens, sparking new and necessary community conversations.

Let's take one last look at *West Side Stories*. It began with a brainstorm between two teenagers who wanted to highlight the rich history of their community before it was too late, and evolved into lessons and learnings that reached audiences through media outlets, college classrooms, and museum spaces. Hernandez developed a lesson about who makes history. Ilten-Gee challenged

taken-for-granted conventions of mapmaking and created a through line from gentrification to Indigenous
rights. The OMCA manifested a physical representation
of *West Side Stories* as an interactive installation that
prompted visitors to reckon with themes of home, land,
and belonging through the voices of those facing the
specter of erasure and eviction—as well as those implicated in the policies and practices of displacement.

Can You Teach AI to Dance? fueled our MIT colleagues'
critical exploration of the affordances and limitations
of computational products that aim to quantify human
creative arts expression. Our Science Gallery Dublin
collaborators used this same project to position young
people as mediators of science and arts learning, while
developing their own understanding of AI as an often-
invisible force even in the most seemingly personal, cultural, and subjective dimensions of our lives.

Integrating the three spheres of criticality, computational thinking, and creative expression does more than
expand the field of engaged learners. CCE unlocks opportunities for practitioners working across a diverse range of
disciplines and settings to reimagine curriculum and pedagogy. Narrowly defined, discipline-specific approaches
can create barriers that block participation. To be transdisciplinary is a robust way to learn. Thanks to colleagues
extending CCE into the social sciences, humanities,
computer and data science, and museum studies, young
people are investigating and advancing diverse disciplines, connecting with one another and communities,

holding power accountable, and developing products and processes that go beyond telling stories of our shared social world as it is. Through their leadership within these experiments at the intersection of civics, science, and art, young people establish a "rightful presence" for themselves across those fields and others.[30] They show us what gives them hope, what needs to change, and the way our world could be.

Epilogue: So You've Read *Code for What?* Now What?

Kyra Kyles, CEO of YR Media

I am reminded of the inequities in the technology industry almost every time I turn on my computer.

Or rather, when I can't.

You see, the so-called facial recognition wizardry that should unlock my sleek, bronze laptop with a mere scan of my face only works if I'm sitting under the brightest of lights. I've been hit with an error message and prompted for my numerical pin if it's even remotely dim where I am. Once my younger sister, who is several shades lighter than I am, was able to lean around me during a particularly frustrating lockout and activate my device with her similar but not identical features.

Perhaps it prefers her light caramel complexion to my medium mocha shade.

Yet my challenges with misidentification are microscopic when compared to the chilling ramifications of other cases of AI ineptitude. For example, in June 2020, the American Civil Liberties Union (ACLU) rallied the public around a wrong having to do with Rekognition, Amazon's controversial cloud-based facial recognition platform. The technology, which was being used by government operatives including US Immigration and Customs Enforcement, resulted in the wrongful arrest of a Black man in the Detroit area who was taken into custody on his own property in front of his wife and young daughters, according to the ACLU, which shared that he spent thirty hours in jail. The incident occurred because of Michigan State Police's use of Rekognition, which coincidentally also misidentified thirty-two members of Congress in its database according to another ACLU test in 2018.[1]

In a more recent case, also in Detroit, a teen girl was ordered out of a roller skating rink because the business's facial recognition system incorrectly identified her as a previous patron who had been involved in a brawl. The problem was that Lamya Robinson had never been to the rink before. Her parents were outraged that the young lady would be put out on the street alone because of an AWOL algorithm.

"You all put my daughter out of the establishment by herself, not knowing what could have happened," her father, Derrick Robinson, told local FOX 2 in an interview. "It just happened to be a blessing that she was calling in frustration to talk to her cousin, but at the same time he pretty much said I'm not that far, let me go see what's wrong with her."[2]

And being tossed from a roller rink is but the tip of the AI iceberg. In addition to these jarring, outrageous examples involving people of color, research from MIT researcher and Algorithmic Justice founder Joy Buolamwini as well as AI guru and industry pioneer Timnit Gebru has highlighted the fact that the software performed the worst for women with darker complexions, so this could foretell both racist and sexist undercurrents within surveillance technology that is becoming more commonplace, even as Microsoft and IBM have absconded from the market, and in June 2020, Reuters reported that Amazon put a pause on enabling police use of Rekognition pending congressional assessment and regulation.[3]

The "white skin as the default" also can disrupt education, one of the so-called equalizers in our society. Amid the pandemic, YR Media—tipped off by a California college student whose friend had been impacted—investigated allegations that pupils with darker complexions were being inaccurately marked as absent or flagged as cheaters due to issues with proctoring software.

The resulting story, "Surveillance U," featured anecdotes from young people of color, including Sergine Beaubrun, who told our YR Media correspondent Zoe Harwood that she "never thought she would have to grab her laptop and stand on a table, putting her face right next to the ceiling light, just to take her mock bar exam. She said that ExamSoft, which is often used to remotely proctor the single most important test a law student will take, had difficulty registering—or even detecting—her face."[4]

Not only did this make Beaubrun question the software, but it made her question her sense of belonging in the legal field.

"It's just like, was this profession really meant for me? The software isn't. It shouldn't have taken me jumping on a table and going this close to light, just so you guys could recognize me," Beaubrun said. "I hope that this profession recognizes me as a person when I enter it."

The problem is that in the same era in which we are heralding private space travel, self-driving automobiles, robot dogs, and AI influencers, we are still contending with age-old remnants of racial discrimination and the (literal) good old (or young) boys club of networking that bars people of color, especially women, from innovative industries. The technology field, from the C-suite to senior management, is extremely white and predominantly male. Even when there are the so-called POCs, few are Black people. How does this show up in practice?

The same way that it does in other industries including entertainment, investment/banking, and finance: the product does not serve the increasingly diverse base of end users, and in fact, is antagonistic toward them.

The facial recognition challenges are a literal example of how homogeneity breeds both invisibility and hypervisibility.

This must end.

Like so many other industries that are indulging in navel-gazing and mostly trying to assuage their guilt with performative efforts (hashtags, social posts, and endless surveys that reveal what we already know), technology needs to perform a deep scan of itself and recognize the problem sitting right in front of its face. The way to solve the problem is by creating the space for those who have been left outside the algorithm for far too long. This means investing in, and drawing from, the many resources that have sprung up to address issues of engagement and representation.

Yes, YR Media is doing the work with a co-led model centered on emerging content creators whose brilliance lights our way. As a longtime advocate of diversity—or as I call it, reality—joining this organization at the beginning of 2020 was a bright spot in a moment of admitted wretchedness, from pandemic to protests for normal human rights for BIPOC individuals. I fully believe that whether team YR is ushering in the next generation of journalists, developers, or music producers, our founder, Ellin O'Leary, set us on a path to disrupt industries that have set up a seemingly intractable pipeline of privilege.

Nearly thirty years later, and with the help and leadership of passionate, determined YR stars (aka youth employees) and staff, we are seeing a shift. But we are one organization. There are so many others pouring into young BIPOC future creators who have every right to take their place in an industry where they so often set the trends. There are entire movements focused on making the tech space not only inclusive but also welcoming. Yes, there is a difference between tolerating and championing.

The onus truly is on these technology companies, which all too often see themselves as "neutral" and therefore blameless in the inequities they help replicate. They want to control, shift the responsibility on the end user, or bemoan societal challenges that they didn't create. Even for would-be allies, it's certainly easier to post about it than to be about it and particularly if that means sacrificing some of your innate privilege for change. It's time for the industry and its superstars to be as embracing of the rising majority as it is of our dollars and social capital.

Tech leaders and stakeholders should be most active in solving a problem that they are causing; every one of us can do something to turn the tide of tech.

To that end, please indulge me as I name-drop some of the many wonderful organizations and outlets pushing for much-needed change. Whether they are illuminating issues or offering training as well as career and moral support, they are taking on tech giants, inequitable trends, and winning.

I am talking about outlets centering and uplifting BIPOC authors and creators in tech, like Afrotech, the Plug, Black Enterprise, Blacks in Technology, Blavity, Capital B, Neufluence, Visible Hands, Score 3 Ventures, and Olin College of Engineering Extending Access to STEM Empowerment Lab. I am talking about youth-serving organizations transforming how we prepare and partner with the next generation of tech makers, including Technovation, the Hidden Genius Project, Black Girls Code, All Star Code, the App ACCelerator, CODE 2040,

GET City Collective, Teen-o-vators, YESTEM Collaborative, MathTalk, BreakFree Education, and Digital Interactive Visual Arts and Sciences for Social Justice. We count on associations like the American Indian Science and Engineering Society, National Society of Black Engineers, Society of Hispanic Professional Engineers, Black and Brown Founders, Digital Undivided, LatinX Startup Alliance, Morehouse School of Medicine S.T.E.A.M. Academy, i.c. stars, Civic Design Studio, and Techqueria to propel emerging innovative leaders and ideas. We count, too, on support from visionary investors like Backstage Capital and world-bending insights from initiatives like Algorithmic Justice League to hold tech accountable and build movements for equity.

My call to action to those who have read these pages so far is to further research this list and build on it. But don't just gaze at them and marvel at their accomplishments. Help fund them. Step up as a volunteer. Share their updates on social media. If it's an outlet, read the stories it writes about underrepresented groups in technology. If it's an incubator or training program, support its alumni along with the businesses and initiatives they create through hiring or patronage. If it's a research collective, cite its scholarly findings. In all cases, amplify them and the solutions that they bring to a pervasive problem.

When we say this must end, we must also act to end it.

Acknowledgments

Our gratitude begins with Asha Richardson, who cofounded the Mobile Action Lab (now YR Interactive) in 2011. Asha led the day-to-day operations of the interactive team until 2018, established its first curriculum, steered production of its debut projects, and set its course to where we are today. None of this work could have been accomplished without her vision, leadership, and commitment to cohort after cohort of young people, who credit Asha with setting them up for excellence. Special thanks also goes out to Radamés Ajna and Marjerrie Masicat, who picked up the baton from Asha and gracefully guided YR Media's interactive team through several of the projects highlighted here.

Thank you to our tremendous YR Media colleagues who, over the course of the organization's quarter-century history and especially the last ten years, contributed directly and indirectly to the processes as well as products described in these pages. Producers, developers, designers, editors, and other experts who shaped interactive projects created in the timeframe of this book include Senay

Alkebulan, Kevin Sosa, Maya Escobar, Isabella Ordaz, Donta Jackson, Storm White, Eli Arbreton, Joi Smith, Lo Béni-chou, Teresa Chin, Ike Sriskandarajah, Rebecca Martin, Nishat Kurwa, Brett Myers, Denise Tejada, Darelle Brown, Rafael Johns, Edgar Romero, Robyn Gee, Paolo Match-ett, Noah Nelson, Chaz Hubbard, Luis Flores, Michael Prizmich, Brandon McFarland, James Rowlands, Jenny Lei Bolario, Ashleigh Kenny, Morgan Siegel, Rosa Terra-zas, Monica Anderson, Ariel Tang, Dante Brundage, Elisa-beth Guta, Jen Tribbet, Marlene Rodriguez, Mila Sutphin, Shanya Wiliams, Deborah Raji, Tree Moses, Edel, Xion Abiodun, Valeria Araujo, Victoria Balla, Zoe Harwood, Dante Ruberto, Bayani Salgado, Noah Villarreal, Ifalola Amin-McCoy, Nimah Gobir, Devin Glover, Renato Russo, Ariam Mogos, Kyle McDonald, Seth Marceau, Dominik Vaughan, Nancy DeVille, Pablo De La Hoya, Peter Disney, Kai Sugioka-Stone, Nicolas Lai, Christy Duong, Desmond Meagley, Hanif Brandy-Mangrai, Kadeem Palcios, Namiye Peoples, Jazon Blasher, Jessica Wang, Gabriel Saravia, Cas-sandra Xiloxochitl Gutierrez, Nyge Turner, Merk Nguyen, Ricardo Perez, Imani Jones, Tiffany Gresseau, Tatiana Cruz, Carissa Wu, Myles Smith, Isaiah Richardson, Jahlil Watson, Charlie Stuip, Arlette Nolasco Sanchez, Christian Mireles, Derrika Pierson, Austin Lai, Valencia White, and Gabriel Browne.

To Ellin O'Leary, the founder and president of YR Media until 2020, and Kyra Kyles, whose leadership is powering YR Media into the future: your shared, bound-less belief in young people as story makers, truth tellers, world builders, and artists is what established the high bar that the interactive team is always shooting for. A million thanks.

We want to call out the crucial work of our colleagues across the organization who apply their talents and labor everyday to create safe, supported conditions for young people's creativity and learning. Huge respect and gratitude to the teams that provide the organization's media education and support services, maintain the beautiful building in downtown Oakland, run the newsroom and national hubs, lead creative services, design and maintain a complex tech infrastructure, produce resources for educators to expand impact, orchestrate our one-of-a-kind music division, craft communications, run finance and operations, and keep the funding coming in. Special thanks to Pedro Vega Jr., whose leadership is carrying interactive into its next chapter.

The first grant to the interactive team came from the John D. and Catherine T. MacArthur Foundation. Thank you for believing in us! Game-changing grants soon followed from the National Science Foundation, Division of Research on Learning, specifically AISL Award #1906895 (Innovative Approaches to Informal Education in Artificial Intelligence); #1647150-AM0005, subaward number UWSC9758 (Science Learning+); #1323791 (NEXT Generation: The Youth Radio Innovation Lab); #1614239 (WAVES: A STEM-Powered Youth News Network for the Nation); and ITEST Award #1513282 (From Data to Awesome [D2A]: Youth Learning to Be Data

Scientists). While grateful for and humbled by this support, we take full responsibility for the views, findings, conclusions, or recommendations expressed in this book—all of which are our own, and do not necessarily reflect those of the National Science Foundation or any other funder.

Led by the CS legend Hal Abelson, our partners at MIT App Inventor were with us when we launched interactive, and—through their radically accessible tools, in the most generous and expansive way—taught both our students and us what it means to code. Along with Hal, we want to thank Selim Tezel, Karen Lang, Josh Sheldon, Marisol Diaz, and Andrew McKinney. One day Tapan Parikh, who was a professor at the University of California at Berkeley at the time, took some grad students on a tour of YR Media, and from there we hatched a multiyear collaboration with Cornell Tech that taught us to tell stories with data. Thank goodness for Ellen Spertus and Drew Mason from Mills College; they immediately rooted for us when we were getting the App Lab off the ground and led our first coding workshops. Sepehr Vakil's excitement about the approach to CS education that we were developing helped us realize that we were onto something. Alex Gurn and Kristin Bass from Rockman et al., a research and evaluation company, have been so much more than evaluators in the traditional sense. Their keen insights have helped to shape the very programs that they have worked so hard to authentically assess. Nimah Gobir's contributions as a producer of the learning environments, media, and research contained in these pages have been crucial. And to our editor at the MIT Press, Susan Buckley: thank you for attending that panel, noticing its potential, initiating a conversation, and then guiding us so wisely through every step in turning those ideas into this book in our hands.

*   *   *

We also want to share our individual thanks.

From Cliff

To my community. To each and every person whom I have had the pleasure of connecting with, or sharing a meal, laughter, walk, dilemma, lesson, revelation, and tear with. You have all had an influence on how I walk in the world. Those moments and lifelong relationships have had an impact on how I think, see, question, sense, and relate with others. And by extension, those memories have all shaped how I experienced, reflected, and wrote this book. Thank you.

All praise and love go to the unrecognized, underappreciated, and too often nameless individuals who work tirelessly for the dispossessed along with those fighting for what Paulo Freire called "the creation of a world in which it will be easier to love."[1]

To my love and life partner, Tyrah Taylor, thank you for holding space for me when I needed a nonjudgmental ear to listen to me process and vent, and your steady, unwavering, and unconditional calm and support. I hope that I can reciprocate with the same level of grace, compassion, and thoughtfulness you exhibit daily. To my son, João Tenzin 樂 然 Lee Ramirez, and daughter, Hayden Naima Taylor, thank you both for bearing with me when I was less than my most patient, thoughtful, and/or compassionate self during quarantine and deadlines that got in the way of game nights, arts and crafts, ice cream trips, and all the fun we have together. An especially heartfelt appreciation goes to my now-teenage son who has consistently served as a sounding board and tester for critical computational ideas in theory and practice. To my parents, Shun and Lily Lee, thank you for your tireless sacrifices and acts of love to provide Cindy and me with the foundations to chase after our passions and dreams.

To my collaborator, mentor, work partner, and friend, Lissa Soep. For the past seven years, you have been a confidant, through the peaks and valleys of my personal and professional journey, and always a friend first and supervisor last. Your understanding, thoughtfulness, meticulousness, care, and vision taught me much about centering my voice in writing, consideration of multiple perspectives, and most important, doing right by our young people. I am so thankful that our paths converged, at the right time and place, and eagerly await future collaborations.

To my dedicated weekly writing partners, Dana Wright, Mike Viola, and Danny Martinez. Thank you for helping me stay accountable, and being excellent thought partners and my sounding board. I've learned immensely with all of y'all throughout this journey.

Big shout-outs to my lifelong mentors from the University of California at Los Angeles and beyond; you strengthened and sharpened my critical educational and research praxis. Thank you Ernest Morrell, Marjorie Orellana-Faulstich, Kris Gutierrez, Jane Margolis, Tyrone Howard, Mike Rose, and Concepcion Valadez. Each of y'all modeled for me what it means to be a humanizing and justice-oriented researcher and educator.

Deep gratitudes to my academic peers who carried me throughout our respective journeys: Antero Garcia, G. Reyes, Elizabeth Montaño, Cueponcaxochtil Moreno, Nicole Mirra, Monique Lane, Tomás Galguera, Wanda Watson, Pedro Nava, Argelia Lara, Jaci Urbani, Jonathan Iris-Wilbanks, Priya Driscoll, Wendi Williams, Raina León, Rebecca Anguiano, Cynthia Martinez, Suzanne Schmidt, Gloria Sosa, Bedford Palmer, Robin Dunn, David Quijada, Cynthia Ganote, Mary Raygoza, Ursula Aldana, Patrick Camangian, Mark Bautista, Ramón Martinez, Mel Bertrand, Jean Ryoo, Jesse Moya, Eréndira Rueda, Rhoda Freelon, and Antonio Martinez.

To my NCTE Cultivating New Voices fellows who provided the community that we so desperately needed, and to our mentors for sharing the path and light they traversed. Thank you Keisha Allen, Steven Alvarez, Donja Bridges, Cati de los Ríos, Sakeena Everett, Marilisa Jimenez Garcia, Roberta Price Gardner, Lorena Gutierrez, Lamar Johnson, Reanae McNeal, Sandra L. Osorio, LaToya

Sawyer, Joanna Wong, Juan Guerra, Eva Lam, Mariana Souto-Manning, Yolando Sealey-Ruiz, Marcelle Haddix, Valerie Kinloch, Carol Lee, Django Paris, Peter Smagorinsky, Susi Long, Sonia Nieto, Anthony Brown, Keffrelyn Brown, Bob Fecho, Sarah Freedman, Sonja Lanehart, Leigh Patel, and Maisha Winn.

Huge thanks to my Mills College Research Justice at the Intersections fellows who gave pointed feedback and thoughtful critique in the early stages of this manuscript. Thank you to Natalee Kēhaulani Bauer, Mozzie DosAlmas, Mario Hernandez, Jimin Kim, Rigoberto Marquéz, Suzanne Schmidt, Dana Wright, and Jane Yamashiro.

Heartfelt appreciation to the many mentors, colleagues, lifelong educators, writers, and researchers I met through the Bay Area and UCLA Writing Project as well as the National Writing Project. The wisdom of Carol Tateishi, Marty Williams, Paul Oh, Christina Cantrill, Elyse Eidman-Aadahl, Lanette Jimerson, and Felicia George, among many others, instilled confidence in me as a teacher, writer, presenter, facilitator, and researcher. Y'all opened my eyes to the importance, complexities, and nuances of multiliteracies—first, through the creation of my own family reunion digital story, and then as a keynote speaker with Asha Richardson at the NWP annual meeting.

To my Life Academy fam that shaped who I am today, as a colleague, friend, mentor, social justice advocate, and lifelong Oakland ridah! I would not be the educator that I am today if we didn't go through hell and back our first years of starting a small, autonomous public school in East Oakland. Our never-ending struggles just made us stronger! Thank you Venus Mesui, Julio Magaña, Yumi Matsui, Toai Dao, Sandy Calvo, Marisa Thompson, Danny Wilcox, Rich Boettner, Carlos Herrera, Steve Miller, Carmelita Reyes, Preston Thomas, Laura Flaxman, Gwen Larsen, Alison McDonald, Sameer Sampat, Candace Hamilton, Micia Mosely, Alicia Gomez, Antonio Acosta, Rebecca Huang, Erik Rice, Fred Ngo, Kim Young, Jill Thomas, Emily Rigotti, Brooke Fitzgerald, Leslie Kawamoto Hsu, Emma Paulino, and Butler.

To all of my former students, I've never learned more about myself and humanizing relationships than in teaching you.

From Lissa

I've been thinking about the earliest days of the App Lab—when it was just Asha and our first youth team, Austin De Rubira and Christian Gonzalez. It took a major leap of faith for Austin and Christian to sign up for a YR internship that didn't even exist yet. As we said often back then, it really did feel like we were launching a little start-up from within an established nonprofit, which meant that half the time, Asha and I were making it up as we went along. Austin and Christian, your willingness to take that creative risk got this whole thing going, and you are cofounders of what we've become. Also vital in those early days of interactive were Asiya Wadud, Jeff Daniel, David Pescovitz, and Akil King, who generously leveraged their prodigious imaginations and networks to unlock key opportunities for our team, and Alexis Madrigal, who, through his own writing and hands-on workshops at YR, has shown us the kind of relevant storytelling with and about technology that we aspire to create. To Joseph Gratz and Bill Sokol, your lawyerly brilliance freed us to think big and be bold because we always knew you had our backs.

For their boundary-breaking framework of "civic imagination," thank you cherished colleagues and friends Henry Jenkins, Sangita Shresthova, and Gabriel Peters-Lazaro, whose memory is a blessing. For the concept of "participatory politics," and the amazing community that formed around it and gave me an intellectual home, thank you Danielle Allen, Cathy Cohen, Jennifer Earl, Elyse Eidman-Aadahl, Howard Gardner, Mimi Ito, Henry Jenkins (again!), Joseph Kahne, and Ethan Zuckerman along with the MacArthur Foundation for bringing us together.

I am beyond grateful for the dear friends I read and write with, who have shaped so very much more than the parts of myself that ever make it to the page: Nicole Fleetwood, Monifa Porter, Sussu Laaksonen, and Rachel Sherman. When I stepped into Youth Radio for the first time in 1999, Beverly Mire, Whiz Ward II, and Ellin O'Leary caught me at a pivotal moment in my professional development, and made all the difference. Rebecca

Martin and Nishat Kurwa, we had the best time, and I learned it all with and from you.

Cliff, people warn you that writing a book together can put strains on even the strongest dynamic between authors. That didn't happen with us. I have never felt anything but huge appreciation and respect for who you are, as a colleague, thinker, educator, activist, and friend, from when you took the job as YR's scholar-in-residence through the final edits of this manuscript. You have modeled for me what it looks like to carry out challenging and vulnerable conversations. You have helped me to see and rethink my own contradictions in ways that I hope will help me to hold myself accountable with compassion for self and others. Our partnership is one of the parts of my professional life that I hold most dear.

Thank you to my parents and siblings, who raised me to cherish the creativity in myself and others. And to my family, Chas, Roma, and Simone: I keep picturing our coffee table, where we eat dinner half the time, watch TV, play cards, have late-night talks and laughing fits, and leave our laundry. It's also where I've put my laptop for many of the writing sessions that have helped produce this book. I like that image of the interlacing of our family life and the work of writing. Thank you for making space for both.

Notes

Foreword

1. Christopher Emdin, *STEM, STEAM, Make, Dream: Reimagining the Culture of Science, Technology, Engineering, and Mathematics* (New York: Houghton Mifflin, 2021).

Chapter 1

1. With the exception of references and direct quotations from published pieces, pseudonyms will be used for all YR Media youth participants.

2. "West Oakland Specific Plans: 4.8 Population, Housing and Employment," accessed November 19, 2021, http://www2.oaklandnet.com /oakca1/groups/ceda/documents/report/oak045563.pdf.

3. Darwin Bondgraham, "Neill Sullivan's Oakland," *East Bay Express*, April 2, 2014; Aaron Glantz, "Report: Investors Buy Nearly Half of Oakland's Foreclosed Homes," *Bay Citizen*, July 23, 2012; Jean Tepperman, "Who's Jacking Up Housing Prices in West Oakland?," *East Bay Express*, October 2, 2013.

4. See also Sarah Van Wart, Kathryn Lanouette, and Tapan S. Parikh, "Scripts and Counterscripts in Community-Based Data Science: Participatory Digital Mapping and the Pursuit of a Third Space," *Journal of the Learning Sciences*, 29, no. 1 (January 2020): 127–153; Sarah Van Wart, Sepehr Vakil, and Tapan S. Parikh, "Apps for Social Justice:

Motivating Computer Science Learning with Design and Real-World Problem Solving" (paper presented at the Conference on Innovation and Technology in Computer Science Education, Uppsala, Sweden, June 23–24, 2014).

5. Maya Escueta, Vincent Quan, Andre Joshua Nickow, and Philip Oreopoulos, "Education Technology: An Evidence-Based Review," National Bureau of Economic Research, August 2017, https://doi.org/10.3386/w23744.

6. Sara Vogel, Rafi Santo, and Dixie Ching, "Visions of Computer Science Education: Unpacking Arguments for and Projected Impacts of CS4All Initiatives," in *Proceedings of the 2017 ACM SIGCSE Technical Symposium on Computer Science Education* (New York: Association for Computing Machinery, 2017), 609–614.

7. Megan Smith, "Computer Science for All," White House, January 30, 2016, https://obamawhitehouse.archives.gov/blog/2016/01/30/computer-science-all.

8. "NYC's Computer Science for All Progress," Fund for Public Schools, February 10, 2021, https://www.fundforpublicschools.org/fps-blog/2021/2/5/cs4all-year5.

9. "Celebrating CS4All's Progress during #CSedweek 2019," Fund for Public Schools, December 13, 2019, https://www.fundforpublicschools.org/fps-blog/2019/12/13/csedweek-2019.

10. "CSEdWeek," accessed November 19, 2021, https://www.csedweek.org/; "Hour of Code," accessed November 19, 2021, https://hourofcode.com/us.

11. Sam Levin, "Sexism, Racism and Bullying Are Driving People out of Tech, US Study Finds," *Guardian*, April 27, 2017, https://www.theguardian.com/technology/2017/apr/27/tech-industry-sexism-racism-silicon-valley-study; Janice Min, "Pinterest and the Subtle Poison of Sexism and Racism in Silicon Valley," *Time*, March 22, 2021, https://time.com/5947561/pinterest-gender-discrimination-racism/.

12. Yolanda A. Rankin, Jakita O. Thomas, and Sheena Erete, "Black Women Speak: Examining Power, Privilege, and Identity in CS Edu-

cation," *ACM Transactions on Computing Education* 21, no. 4 (2021): 1–31.

13. Enora R. Brown, "Freedom for Some, Discipline for 'Others': The Structure of Inequity in Education," in *Education as Enforcement: The Militarization and Corporatization of Schools*, ed. Kenneth J. Saltman and David A. Gabbard (New York: Routledge, 2010), 146–180; Linda Darling-Hammond, *The Flat World and Education: How America's Commitment to Equity Will Determine Our Future* (New York: Teachers College Press, 2015); Oliver P. Hauser, Gordon T. Kraft-Todd, David G. Rand, Martin A. Nowak, and Michael I. Norton, "Invisible Inequality Leads to Punishing the Poor and Rewarding the Rich," *Behavioural Public Policy* (2019): 1–21.

14. Gary Orfield and Chungmei Lee, "Why Segregation Matters: Poverty and Educational Inequality," Civil Rights Project at Harvard University, 2005; Joel Spring, *Deculturalization and the Struggle for Equality: A Brief History of the Education of Dominated Cultures in the United States* (Milton Park, UK: Routledge, 2016); Angela Valenzuela and Brenda Rubio, "Subtractive Schooling," in *The TESOL Encyclopedia of English Language Teaching*, ed. John I. Liontas (Hoboken, NJ: Wiley Blackwell, 2018), 1–7.

15. Sepehr Vakil, "Ethics, Identity, and Political Vision: Toward a Justice-Centered Approach to Equity in Computer Science Education," *Harvard Educational Review* 88, no. 1 (2018): 26–52; Jean J. Ryoo, Alicia Morris, and Jane Margolis, "'What Happens to the Raspado Man in a Cash-Free Society?': Teaching and Learning Socially Responsible Computing," *ACM Transactions on Computing Education* 21, no. 4 (2021): 1–28.

16. Pratim Sengupta, Amanda Dickes, and Amy Farris, "Toward a Phenomenology of Computational Thinking in STEM Education," *Computational Thinking in the STEM Disciplines* (2018): 49–72.

17. Simone Browne, *Dark Matters: On the Surveillance of Blackness* (Durham, NC: Duke University Press, 2015).

18. Angela Calabrese Barton and Edna Tan, "Designing for Rightful Presence in STEM: The Role of Making Present Practices," *Journal of the*

Learning Sciences 28, no. 4–5 (October 20, 2019): 616–658, https://doi
.org/10.1080/10508406.2019.1591411.

19. Ruha Benjamin, "Race after Technology: Abolitionist Tools for
the New Jim Code," *Social Forces* 98, no. 4 (June 2020): 1–3; Cathy
O'Neil, *Weapons of Math Destruction: How Big Data Increases Inequality
and Threatens Democracy* (New York: Crown, 2016); Tonya Mosley,
"Tech Ethicist Tristan Harris Says 'Digital Democracy' Is Needed to
Correct 'a System of Harms,'" WBUR, February 8, 2021; Safiya Umoja
Noble, *Algorithms of Oppression: How Search Engines Reinforce Racism*
(New York: New York University Press, 2018); Douglas Rushkoff and
Leland Purvis, *Program or Be Programmed: Ten Commands for a Digital
Age* (Berkeley: Soft Skull Press, 2011).

20. Yasmin B. Kafai and Kylie A. Peppler, "Transparency Reconsid-
ered: Creative, Critical, and Connected Making with E-Textiles," in
DIY Citizenship: Critical Making and Social Media, ed. Matt Ratto and
Megan Boler (Cambridge, MA: MIT Press, 2014), 179–188; Nicholas
Diakopoulos, "Algorithmic Accountability Reporting: On the Inves-
tigation of Black Boxes," Tow Center for Digital Journalism, Columbia
University, 2014, https://doi.org/10.7916/D8ZK5TW2.

21. Virginia Eubanks, *Automating Inequality: How High-Tech Tools Profile, Police, and Punish the Poor* (New York: St. Martin's Press, 2017).

22. Noble, *Algorithms of Oppression.*

23. Joy Buolamwini and Timnit Gebru, "Gender Shades: Intersectional Accuracy Disparities in Commercial Gender Classification,"
in *Proceedings of Machine Learning Research* 81 (2018): 1–15, https://
proceedings.mlr.press/v81/buolamwini18a/buolamwini18a.pdf.

24. Bobby Allyn, "'The Computer Got It Wrong': How Facial Recognition Led to False Arrest of Black Man," NPR, June 24, 2020,
https://www.npr.org/2020/06/24/882683463/the-computer-got-it
-wrong-how-facial-recognition-led-to-a-false-arrest-in-michig.

25. Benjamin, "Race after Technology," 23.

26. Sheena Vaidyanathan, "Computer Science Goes beyond Coding,"
EdSurge, December 2, 2015, https://www.edsurge.com/news/2015-12
-02-computer-science-goes-beyond-coding.

27. Lisa Delpit, *Other People's Children: Cultural Conflict in the Classroom* (New York: New Press, 2006).

28. Perhaps not surprisingly, we even worked with a youth team at YR Media to create an entire web-based interactive project about biases perpetuated by school dress codes, as you will see in chapter 5.

29. Tomi Dufva and Mikko Dufva, "Metaphors of Code: Structuring and Broadening the Discussion on Teaching Kids to Code," *Thinking Skills and Creativity* 22 (December 2016): 97–110, https://doi.org/10.1016/j.tsc.2016.09.004.

30. Lawrence Lessig, "Rendering Sensible Salient," *Good Society* 27, no. 1–2 (2019): 171–178; Pratim Sengupta, Amanda Dickes, and Amy Voss Farris, *Voicing Code in STEM: A Dialogical Imagination* (Cambridge, MA: MIT Press, 2021); Shirin Vossoughi, Paula K. Hooper, and Meg Escudé, "Making through the Lens of Culture and Power: Toward Transformative Visions for Educational Equity," *Harvard Educational Review* 86, no. 2 (2016): 206–232; Sheena Erete, Karla Thomas, Denise Nacu, Jessa Dickinson, Naomi Thompson, and Nichole Pinkard, "Applying a Transformative Justice Approach to Encourage the Participation of Black and Latina Girls in Computing," *ACM Transactions on Computing Education* 21, no. 4 (2021): 1–24.

31. For more on the history of Youth Radio, see Elisabeth Soep and Vivian Chávez, *Drop That Knowledge: Youth Radio Stories* (Berkeley: University of California Press, 2010).

32. TV Tropes, "Ayiti: The Cost of Life (Video Game)," accessed November 19, 2021, https://tvtropes.org/pmwiki/pmwiki.php/VideoGame/AyitiTheCostOfLife.

33. Jane Margolis, Rachel Estrella, Joanna Goode, Jennifer Jellison Holme, and Kim Nao, *Stuck in the Shallow End: Education, Race, and Computing* (Cambridge, MA: MIT Press, 2017).

34. Clifford Lee, "Re-Mastering the Master's Tools: Recognizing and Affirming the Life Experiences and Cultural Practices of Urban Youth in Critical Computational Literacy through a Video Game Project," University of California at Los Angeles, 2012, https://escholarship.org/uc/item/99j0t9nj.

35. Clifford H. Lee and and Antero D. Garcia, "'I Want Them to Feel the Fear . . .': Critical Computational Literacy as the New Multimodal Composition," in *Exploring Multimodal Composition and Digital Writing*, ed. Richard E. Ferdig and Kristine E. Pytash (Hershey, PA: IGI Global, 2014), 364–378.

Chapter 2

1. For selected publications, see Youth and Participatory Politics, accessed May 31, 2021, https://ypp.dmlcentral.net/. The network members were Danielle Allen, Cathy Cohen, Jennifer Earl, Elyse Eidman-Aadahl, Howard Gardner, Mimi Ito, Henry Jenkins, Joseph Kahne, and Ethan Zuckerman. See also Mimi Ito, Richard Arum, Dalton Conley, Kris D. Gutiérrez, Ben Kirshner, Sonia Livingstone, Vera Michalchik, et al., *The Connected Learning Research Network: Reflections on a Decade of Engaged Scholarship* (Irvine, CA: Connected Learning Alliance, 2020); Brigid Barron, Kimberley Gomez, Nichole Pinkard, and Caitlin K. Martin, *The Digital Youth Network* (Cambridge, MA: MIT Press, 2014); S. Craig Watkins, *Don't Knock the Hustle: Young Creatives, Tech Ingenuity, and the Making of a New Innovation Economy* (Boston, MA: Beacon Press, 2019); Henry Jenkins, Gabriel Peters-Lazaro, and Sangita Shresthova, *Popular Culture and the Civic Imagination: Case Studies of Creative Social Change* (New York: NYU Press, 2020); Sam Mejias, Naomi Thompson, Raul Mishael Sedas, Mark Rosin, Elisabeth Soep, Kylie Peppler, Joseph Roche, et al., "The Trouble with STEAM and Why We Use It Anyway," *Science Education* 105 (2021): 209–231.

2. Jane Margolis, Jean J. Ryoo, Cueponcaxochitl D. M. Sandoval, Clifford Lee, Joanna Goode, and Gail Chapman, "Beyond Access: Broadening Participation in High School Computer Science," *ACM Inroads* 3, no. 4 (2012): 72–78.

3. Paulo Freire, *Pedagogy of the Oppressed* (New York: Continuum, 1996).

4. Valerie J. Shute, Chen Sun, and Jodi Asbell-Clarke, "Demystifying Computational Thinking," *Educational Research Review* 22 (2017): 142–158; Alfred V. Aho, "Ubiquity Symposium: Computation and Computational Thinking," *Ubiquity* (January 2011), https://doi.org/10.1145/1895419.1922682.

5. Jeannette M. Wing, "Computational Thinking," *Communications of the ACM* 49, no. 3 (March 2006): 33–35.

6. Linda Darling-Hammond, "Race, Inequality and Educational Accountability: The Irony of 'No Child Left Behind,'" *Race Ethnicity and Education* 10, no. 3 (October 2007): 245–260.

7. Edward B. Fiske, *Champions of Change: The Impact of the Arts on Learning* (Washington, DC: Arts Education Partnership, 1999); Jame S. Catterall, Susan A. Dumais, and Gillian Hampden-Thompson, *The Arts and Achievement in At-Risk Youth: Findings from Four Longitudinal Studies*, Research Report # 55 (Washington, DC: National Endowment for the Arts, 2012); Rubén A. Gaztambide-Fernández, "Why the Arts Don't Do Anything: Toward a New Vision for Cultural Production in Education," *Harvard Educational Review* 83, no. 1 (April 2003): 211–237.

8. Mejias et al., "The Trouble with STEAM."

9. Anne Bamford, *The Wow Factor: Global Research Compendium on the Impact of the Arts in Education* (Kornwestheim, Germany: Waxmann Verlag, 2006).

10. Ellen Winner, Lois Hetland, Shirley Veenema, Kim Sheridan, and Patricia Palmer, "Studio Thinking: How Visual Arts Teaching Can Promote Disciplined Habits of Mind," in *New Directions in Aesthetics, Creativity, and the Arts*, ed. Paul Locher, Colin Martindale, and Leonid Dorfman (Amityville, NY: Baywood Publishing Co., 2006), 189–205; Shirin Vossoughi, Paula K. Hooper, and Meg Escudé, "Making through the Lens of Culture and Power: Towards Transformative Visions for Educational Equity," *Harvard Educational Review* 86, no. 2 (June 2016): 206–232; Cherise Martinez-McBride, "Tinkering as Digital Equity Practice: Defining and Designing Digital Pedagogy with Learning in Mind," *International Journal of Information and Learning Technology* (under review); Erica Halverson, *How the Arts Can Save Education* (New York: Teachers College Press, 2021); Raquel Jimenez, "Creating to Connect: Understanding Community Arts Education and Efforts to Educate a New Generation of Citizen Artists" (PhD diss., Harvard University, 2021); Edmund S. Adjapong and Christopher Emdin, "Rethinking Pedagogy in Urban Spaces: Implementing Hip-Hop Pedagogy in the Urban Science Classroom," *Journal of Urban Learning, Teaching, and Research* 11 (January 2015): 66–77.

11. Native Land Digital, "Welcome," accessed November 19, 2021, https://native-land.ca/.

12. "Land Acknowledgement," accessed November 19, 2021, https://land.codeforanchorage.org/.

13. John Maeda and Red Burns, "Creative Code," *Education* 7 (2005): 177; Kylie Peppler and Yasmin Kafai, "Creative Coding: Programming for Personal Expression," accessed on November 19, 2021, https://citeseerx.ist.psu.edu/viewdoc/download?doi=10.1.1.88.1191&rep=rep1&type=pdf; Deena Engel and Joanna Phillips, "Applying Conservation Ethics to the Examination and Treatment of Software- and Computer-Based Art," *Journal of the American Institute for Conservation* 58, no. 3 (July 3, 2019): 180–195, https://doi.org/10.1080/01971360.2019.1598124; "Mycelium," accessed November 19, 2021, https://onecm.com/projects/mycelium/; Kylie Peppler, "STEAM-Powered Computing Education: Using E-Textiles to Integrate the Arts and STEM," *Computer* 46, no. 9 (2013): 38–43; William Christopher Payne, Yoav Bergner, Mary Etta West, Carlie Charp, R. Benjamin Shapiro, Danielle Albers Szafir, Edd V. Taylor, and Kayla DesPortes, "DanceON: Culturally Responsive Creative Computing," in *Proceedings of the 2021 CHI Conference on Human Factors in Computing Systems* (New York: Association for Computing Machinery, 2021), 1–16; Dionne N. Champion, "The STEAM Dance Makerspace: A Context for Integration: An Investigation of Learning at the Intersections of STEM, Art, Making and Embodiment" (PhD diss., Northwestern University, 2018); Dionne N. Champion, Eli Tucker-Raymond, Amon Millner, Brian Gravel, Christopher G. Wright, Rasheda Likely, Ayana Allen-Handy, and Tikyna M. Dandridge, "(Designing for) Learning Computational STEM and Arts Integration in Culturally Sustaining Learning Ecologies," *Information and Learning Sciences* (2020), accessed January 23, 2022, https://www.researchgate.net/publication/346427868_Designing_for_learning_computational_STEM_and_arts_integration_in_culturally_sustaining_learning_ecologies; Amon Millner and Edward Baafi, "Modkit: Blending and Extending Approachable Platforms for Creating Computer Programs and Interactive Objects," in *Proceedings of the 10th International Conference on Interaction Design and Children* (New York: Association for Computing Machinery, 2011), 250–253.

14. Jeffrey M. R. Duncan-Andrade and Ernest Morrell, *The Art of Critical Pedagogy: Possibilities for Moving from Theory to Practice in Urban Schools* (New York: Peter Lang, 2008); Nicole Mirra, Ernest Morrell, and Danielle Filipiak, "From Digital Consumption to Digital Invention: Toward a New Critical Theory and Practice of Multiliteracies," *Theory into Practice* 57, no. 1 (2018): 12–19; Dipti Desai and David Darts, "Interrupting Everyday Life: Public Interventionist Art as Critical Public Pedagogy," *International Journal of Art and Design Education* 35, no. 2 (2016): 183–195; Sadia Habib, "Art, Social Justice and Critical Pedagogy in Educational Research: The Portrait of an Artist as a Young Person," in *Handbook of Qualitative Research in Education*, ed. Michael R. M. Ward and Sara Delamont (Cheltenham, UK: Edward Elgar Publishing, 2020), 360–373; Bettina L. Love, "A Ratchet Lens: Black Queer Youth, Agency, Hip-hop, and the Black Ratchet Imagination," *Educational Researcher* 46, no. 9 (2017): 539–547; David Stovall, "We Can Relate: Hip-hop Culture, Critical Pedagogy, and the Secondary Classroom," *Urban Education* 41, no. 6 (2006): 585–602; Kristen P. Goessling, Dana E. Wright, Amanda C. Wager, and Marit Dewhurst, eds., *Engaging Youth in Critical Arts Pedagogies and Creative Research for Social Justice: Opportunities and Challenges of Arts-Based Work and Research with Young People* (London: Routledge, 2021); Marit Dewhurst, *Social Justice Art: A Framework for Activist Art Pedagogy* (Cambridge, MA: Harvard Education Press, 2014); Aaron D. Knochel and Ryan M. Patton, "If Art Education Then Critical Digital Making: Computational Thinking and Creative Code," *Studies in Art Education* 57, no. 1 (2015): 21–38; Dana Cuff, Anastasia Loukaitou-Sideris, Todd Presner, Maite Zubiaurre, and Jonathan Jae-an Crisman, *Urban Humanities: New Practices for Reimagining the City* (Cambridge, MA: MIT Press, 2020).

15. Henry Jenkins, Gabriel Peters-Lazaro, and Sangita Shresthova, eds., *Popular Culture and the Civic Imagination: Case Studies of Creative Social Change* (New York: NYU Press, 2019).

16. Knochel and Patton, "If Art Education Then Critical Digital Making."

17. "John Dewey My Pedagogic Creed," accessed November 19, 2021, http://dewey.pragmatism.org/creed.htm.

18. John Hurley Flavell, *The Developmental Psychology of Jean Piaget* (New York: Van Nostrand Publishing, 1963), https://doi.org/10.1037 /11449-000; Edutopia, "Project-Based Learning: A Short History," accessed November 19, 2021, https://www.edutopia.org/project-based -learning-history; Idit Harel and Seymour Papert, eds., *Construction-ism* (Norwood, NJ: Ablex Publishing, 1991).

19. Joseph S. Krajcik and Phyllis C. Blumenfeld, "Project-Based Learning," in *The Cambridge Handbook of the Learning Sciences*, ed. R. Keith Sawyer (Cambridge: Cambridge University Press, 2006), 317–333.

20. Etienne Wenger, "Communities of Practice: A Brief Introduction," 2011, http://hdl.handle.net/1794/11736.

21. Jean Lave and Etienne Wenger, *Situated Learning: Legitimate Peripheral Participation* (Cambridge: Cambridge University Press, 1991); Manuel Luis Espinoza, Shirin Vossoughi, Mike Rose, and Luis S. Poza, "Matters of Participation: Notes on the Study of Dignity and Learning," *Mind, Culture, and Activity* 27, no. 4 (2020): 325–347; https://doi.org/10 .1080/10749039.2020.1779304.

22. Nicole Mirra, Antero Garcia, and Ernest Morrell, *Doing Youth Participatory Action Research: Transforming Inquiry with Researchers, Educators, and Students* (Milton Park, UK: Routledge, 2015).

23. Youthprise, "Youth Participatory Action Research Toolkit," accessed November 20, 2021, https://youthprise.org/ypar-toolkit/.

24. Antwi Akom, Aekta Shah, Aaron Nakai, and Tessa Cruz, "Youth Participatory Action Research (YPAR) 2.0: How Technological Innovation and Digital Organizing Sparked a Food Revolution in East Oakland," *International Journal of Qualitative Studies in Education* 29, no. 10 (2016): 1287–1307.

25. Akom et al., "Youth Participatory Action Research"; Julio Cammarota and Michelle Fine, eds., *Revolutionizing Education: Youth Participatory Action Research in Motion* (New York: Routledge, 2010); Jason Corburn "Combining Community-Based Research and Local Knowledge to Confront Asthma and Subsistence-Fishing Hazards in Greenpoint/Williamsburg, Brooklyn, New York," *Environmental Health Perspectives* 110, suppl. 2 (2002): 241–248.

26. Akom et al., "Youth Participatory Action Research."

27. Patrick Camangian and Stephanie Cariaga, "Social and Emotional Learning Is Hegemonic Miseducation: Students Deserve Humanization Instead," *Race Ethnicity and Education* (2021): 1–21.

28. bell hooks, *Sisters of the Yam: Black Women and Self-Recovery* (Boston: South End Press, 1993).

29. Duncan-Andrade and Morrell, *The Art of Critical Pedagogy*.

30. Shirin Vossoughi, Ava Jackson, Megan Bang, Beth Warren, Ann S. Rosebery, and Thomas Philip, "Attunements to the Ethical in Design and Learning," in *Proceedings of International Conference of the Learning Sciences, ICLS* (International Society of the Learning Sciences, June 2018), 1283–1289.

Chapter 3

1. Thomas M. Philip, Maria C. Olivares-Pasillas, and Janet Rocha, "Becoming Racially Literate about Data and Data-Literate about Race: Data Visualizations in the Classroom as a Site of Racial-Ideological Micro-Contestations," *Cognition and Instruction* 34, no. 4 (2016): 361–388.

2. Wil van der Aalst, "Data Science in Action," in *Process Mining: Data Science in Action* (Berlin: Springer, 2016), 3–23; Valerie J. Shute, Chen Sun, and Jodi Asbell-Clarke, "Demystifying Computational Thinking," *Educational Research Review* 22 (November 2017): 142–158.

3. "The Bob Fitch Photography Archive Movements for Change," Stanford Libraries, Stanford University, accessed October 8, 2020, https://exhibits.stanford.edu/fitch/browse/black-panther-party -oakland-california-1968-1972?page=5&per_page=10.

4. "Oakland, California Population 2021 (Demographics, Maps, Graphs)," accessed November 20, 2021, https://worldpopulationreview .com/us-cities/oakland-ca-population; "Explore Census Data," accessed November 20, 2021, https://data.census.gov/cedsci/table?g=1600000 US0653000&tid=ACSDT1Y2019.B03002.

5. "Bay Area Census—City of Antioch—1970–1990 Census Data," accessed November 20, 2021, http://www.bayareacensus.ca.gov/cities /Antioch70.htm; "Explore Census Data," accessed November 20, 2021, https://data.census.gov/cedsci/table?q=antioch,%20ca&tid=ACSD P1Y2015.DP05&hidePreview=false; Lauren Hepler, "The Hidden Toll of California's Black Exodus," *CalMatters*, July 15, 2020, Economy sec., http://calmatters.org/projects/california-black-population-exodus/.

6. Nicole Montojo, Eli Moore, and Nicole Mauri, "Roots, Race, and Place: A History of Racially Exclusionary Housing in the San Francisco Bay Area," Othering and Belonging Institute, October 2, 2019, https://belonging.berkeley.edu/rootsraceplace.

Chapter 4

1. Chimamanda Ngozi Adichie, *The Danger of a Single Story*, filmed in 2009, TED video, 18:38, https://www.ted.com/talks/chimamanda _ngozi_adichie_the_danger_of_a_single_story.

2. "West Side Stories," accessed November 18, 2021, https://youth radio.github.io/.

3. "West Side Stories."

4. "West Side Stories."

5. "Common Sense Census," Common Sense Media, accessed November 18, 2021, https://www.commonsensemedia.org/research/the-com mon-sense-census-media-use-by-tweens-and-teens-2019.

6. "The State of Mental Health in America," accessed November 18, 2021, https://www.mhanational.org/issues/state-mental-health-america; Mizuko Ito, Candice Odgers, and Stephen Schueller, "Social Media and Youth Wellbeing Report," Connected Learning Alliance, accessed November 18, 2021, https://clalliance.org/wp-content/uploads/2020/06 /Social-Media-and-Youth-Wellbeing-Report.pdf.

7. Paulo Freire, *Pedagogy of the Oppressed* (New York: Continuum, 1996).

8. Freire, *Pedagogy of the Oppressed*.

9. "Transgender Law Center," accessed November 18, 2021, https://transgenderlawcenter.org/legalinfo; "GSA Network," accessed November 18, 2021, https://gsanetwork.org/resources/.

10. Maureen M. Black and Ambika Krishnakumar, "Children in Low-Income, Urban Settings: Interventions to Promote Mental Health and Well-being," *American Psychologist* 53, no. 6 (June 1998): 635–646.

11. Corinne David-Ferdon, Thomas R. Simon, and Alida Knuth, "Preventing Youth Violence: Opportunities for Action," National Center for Injury Prevention and Control, Centers for Disease Control and Prevention, June 2014, 1–54.

12. Naomi Priest, Yin Paradies, Brigid Trenerry, Mandy Truong, Saffron Karlsen, and Yvonne Kelly, "A Systematic Review of Studies Examining the Relationship between Reported Racism and Health and Wellbeing for Children and Young People," *Social Science and Medicine* 95 (2013): 115–127; Lee M. Pachter, Cleopatra H. Caldwell, James S. Jackson, and Bruce A. Bernstein, "Discrimination and Mental Health in a Representative Sample of African-American and Afro-Caribbean Youth," *Journal of Racial and Ethnic Health Disparities* 5, no. 4 (2018): 831–837; Byron L. Dorgan, "The Tragedy of Native American Youth Suicide," *Psychological Services* 7, no. 3 (2010): 213–218; Krista M. Malott and Tina R. Paone, "Stressors and Barriers for Latino/a Youth," in *Group Activities for Latino/a Youth: Strengthening Identities and Resiliencies through Counseling*, ed. Krista M. Malott and Tina R. Paone (Milton Park, UK: Taylor and Francis Group, 2016), 15–34; David R. Williams, "Stress and the Mental Health of Populations of Color: Advancing Our Understanding of Race-Related Stressors," *Journal of Health and Social Behavior* 59, no. 4 (2018): 466–485; Carol Dashiff, Wendy DiMicco, Beverly Myers, and Kathy Sheppard, "Poverty and Adolescent Mental Health," *Journal of Child and Adolescent Psychiatric Nursing* 22, no. 1 (2009): 23–32.

13. Dexter R. Voisin, Sadiq Patel, Jun Sung Hong, Lois Takahashi, and Noni Gaylord-Harden, "Behavioral Health Correlates of Exposure to Community Violence among African-American Adolescents in Chicago," *Children and Youth Services Review* 69 (2016): 97–105.

14. Tara J. Yosso, "Whose Culture Has Capital? A Critical Race Theory Discussion of Community Cultural Wealth," *Race Ethnicity and Education* 8, no. 1 (2005): 69–91.

15. Yosso, "Whose Culture Has Capital?"

16. Yosso, "Whose Culture Has Capital?"

17. Juan Gómez-Quiñones, "The First Steps: Chicano Labor Conflict and Organizing, 1900–1920," *Aztlan* 3, no. 1 (1973): 13–49; Juan Gómez-Quiñones, *Roots of Chicano Politics, 1600–1940* (Albuquerque: University of New Mexico Press, 1994); Herbert Gutman, *The Black Family in Slavery and Freedom, 1750–1925* (New York: Pantheon Books, 1976); Brenda E. Stevenson, *Life in Black and White: Family and Community in the Slave South* (New York: Oxford University Press, 1996); Lani Guinier, Michelle Fine, and Jane Balin, *Becoming Gentlemen: Women, Law School, and Institutional Change* (Boston: Beacon Press, 1997); Concha Delgado-Gaitan, *The Power of Community: Mobilizing for Family and Schooling* (Boulder, CO: Rowman and Littlefield Publishers, 2001).

18. Jonathan A. Obar and Anne Oeldorf-Hirsch, "The Biggest Lie on the Internet: Ignoring the Privacy Policies and Terms of Service Policies of Social Networking Services," *Information, Communication and Society* 23, no. 1 (2020): 128–147; "Ledger of Harms," Center for Humane Technology, accessed November 19, 2021, https://ledger .humanetech.com/.

19. "Memory Project—Little Rock Central High School National Historic Site (U.S. National Park Service)," accessed November 20, 2021, https://www.nps.gov/chsc/learn/education/memory-project.htm.

20. "Youth Radio: Little Rock 9 Live," accessed November 20, 2021, https://yr.media/littlerock9/; YR Media (@itsYRmedia), "Relive What the Little Rock Nine Went through the Day They Made History," https://twitter.com/i/events/912399126662230016?ref_src=twsrc%5E tfw%7Ctwcamp%5Emoment&ref_url=https%3A%2F%2Fyr.media%2 Flittlerock9%2F.

21. WPSU, "Reliving The Little Rock 9, 60 Years Later," NPR, September 25, 2017, https://radio.wpsu.org/2017-09-25/reliving-the-little-rock -9-60-years-later.

22. Teju Cole, "A True Picture of Black Skin," *New York Times Magazine*, February 18, 2015, https://www.nytimes.com/2015/02/22/magazine/a -true-picture-of-black-skin.html. More recently, web cameras from Hewlett-Packard came under fire when its face recognition tool was unable to detect Black faces. Beyond the engineers and inventors who created tools without consideration of dark-skinned people are the numerous examples of "editorial licenses" to manipulate Black faces for their purposes, such as *Time* magazine's darkening of O. J. Simpson's mug shot or the lightening of Black faces in advertisements.

23. CS Unplugged, accessed November 20, 2021, https://www.csun plugged.org/en/.

24. Django Paris, "Culturally Sustaining Pedagogy: A Needed Change in Stance, Terminology, and Practice," *Educational Researcher* 41, no. 3 (2012): 93–97.

Chapter 5

1. Sayre Quevedo, "Double Charged: Does Paying Back Victims Cost Kids Their Futures?," YR Media, July 7, 2014, https://yr.media/news /double-charged-how-restoring-victims-complicates-reforming-young -offenders/.

2. "Update: Alameda County Will Stop Collecting Juvenile Fees," YR Media, April 8, 2016, https://yr.media/news/update-alameda-county -will-stop-collecting-juvenile-fees/.

3. Kate Weisburd, email message to YR Media, 2015.

4. "Fines and Fees Justice Center," accessed November 18, 2021, https:// finesandfeesjusticecenter.org/articles/california-sb-190-juveniles/.

5. Jaymie Arns, "Undressing the Dress Codes: An Analysis of Gender in High School Dress Code Policies" (master's thesis, California State University, 2017); Amber Thomas, "The Sexualized Messages Dress Codes Are Sending to Students," *Pudding*, February 2019, https://pudding.cool /2019/02/dress-code-sexualization/; Al Baker, "Baring Shoulders and Knees, Students Protest a Dress Code," *New York Times*, June 6, 2012, https://www.nytimes.com/2012/06/07/nyregion/stuyvesant-high

-school-students-protest-dress-code.html; Brittney McNamara, "Teen's Teacher Reportedly Said She Violated Dress Code Because She's 'Busty' and 'Plus Size,'" *Teen Vogue*, September 11, 2017, https://www .teenvogue.com/story/dress-code-busty; Alyssa Pavlakis and Rachel Roegman, "How Dress Codes Criminalize Males and Sexualize Females of Color," *Phi Delta Kappan* 100, no. 2 (October 2018): 54–58, https:// doi.org/10.1177/0031721718803572; Molly Knefel, "Can We Fix the Race Problem in America's School Discipline?," *Rolling Stone*, January 24, 2014, https://www.rollingstone.com/politics/politics-news/can-we -fix-the-race-problem-in-americas-school-discipline-101922/; Kayla Lattimore, "When Black Hair Violates the Dress Code," NPR, July 17, 2017, https://www.npr.org/sections/ed/2017/07/17/534448313/when -black-hair-violates-the-dress-code.

6. Arns, "Undressing the Dress Codes."

7. Thomas, "The Sexualized Messages Dress Codes Are Sending to Students."

8. Samantha M. Goodin, Alyssa Van Denburg, Sarah K. Murnen, and Linda Smolak, "'Putting on' Sexiness: A Content Analysis of the Presence of Sexualizing Characteristics in Girls' Clothing," *Sex Roles* 65, no. 1–2 (July 2011): 1–12, https://doi.org/10.1007/s11199-011-9966-8.

9. Barbara L. Fredrickson, Tomi-Ann Roberts, Stephanie M. Noll, Diane M. Quinn, and Jean M. Twenge, "That Swimsuit Becomes You: Sex Differences in Self-Objectification, Restrained Eating, and Math Performance," *Journal of Personality and Social Psychology* 75, no. 1 (1998): 269–284, https://doi.org/10.1037/0022-3514.75.1.269; Barbara L. Fredrickson and Tomi-Ann Roberts, "Objectification Theory: Toward Understanding Women's Lived Experiences and Mental Health Risks," *Psychology of Women Quarterly* 21, no. 2 (1997): 173–206; Marika Tiggemann and Amy Slater, "The Role of Self-Objectification in the Mental Health of Early Adolescent Girls: Predictors and Consequences," *Journal of Pediatric Psychology* 40, no. 7 (August 2015): 704–711, https://doi .org/10.1093/jpepsy/jsv021.

10. Courtney Pomeroy, "Boy Sent Home from Private School in Orange County Due to Dreadlocks," News Channel 9, August 14, 2018,

https://newschannel9.com/news/nation-world/boy-sent-home-from
-private-school-in-orange-county-due-to-dreadlocks; Amira Rasool, "A
Black Student Was Reportedly Sent Home from Christ the King Elementary School for Wearing Box Braids," *Teen Vogue*, August 21, 2018,
https://www.teenvogue.com/story/black-student-box-braids-sent-home
-christ-the-king-elementary-school.

11. Hannah Cornejo, "What If You Ruled the School Dress Code?,"
YR Media, April 16, 2019, https://yr.media/news/what-if-you-ruled-the
-school-dress-code/.

12. Cornejo, "What If You Ruled the Dress Code?"

13. Anne E. Adams, Jerine Pegg, and Melissa Case, "Anticipation
Guides: Reading for Mathematics Understanding," *Mathematics Teacher*
108, no. 7 (March 2015): 498–504, https://doi.org/10.5951/math
teacher.108.7.0498; Alice A. Kozen, Rosemary K. Murray, and Idajean
Windell, "Increasing All Students' Chance to Achieve: Using and
Adapting Anticipation Guides with Middle School Learners," *Interven-
tion in School and Clinic* 41, no. 4 (March 2006): 195–200, https://doi
.org/10.1177/10534512060410040101; Katherine A. Dougherty Stahl,
"Proof, Practice, and Promise: Comprehension Strategy Instruction in
the Primary Grades," *Reading Teacher* 57, no. 7 (2004): 598–609.

14. Ciara Nugent, "Pledges Reach Almost $1 Billion to Rebuild Paris'
Notre Dame Cathedral," *Time*, August 17, 2019, https://time.com
/5571518/notre-dame-donations/.

15. "Hurricane Maria," United States Chamber of Commerce Foundation, accessed November 18, 2021, https://www.uschamberfoundation
.org/aid-event/hurricane-maria.

16. "A Commitment to Philanthropy," Giving Pledge, accessed
November 18, 2021, https://givingpledge.org/.

17. Abha Bhattarai, "Thousands of Amazon Workers Receive Food
Stamps. Now Bernie Sanders Wants the Company to Pay Up," *Washington Post*, August 23, 2018, https://www.washingtonpost.com/business
/2018/08/24/thousands-amazon-workers-receive-food-stamps-now
-bernie-sanders-wants-amazon-pay-up/; Paige Leskin, "Here's How

Much Amazon CEO Jeff Bezos, the Richest Person in the World, Has Personally Given to Charity," *Business Insider*, March 4, 2020, https://www.businessinsider.com/jeff-bezos-amazon-how-much-donations-charity-2019-5.

Chapter 6

1. Nyge Turner and Merk Nguyen, "Robots Taking Over This ISH," *Adult ISH* (podcast), produced by YR Media, April 30, 2020, https://yr.media/podcasts/robots-taking-over-this-ish/.

2. Turner and Nguyen, "Robots Taking Over This ISH."

3. Sam Mejias, Naomi Thompson, Raul Mishael Sedas, Mark Rosin, Elisabeth Soep, Kylie Peppler, Joseph Roche, et al., "The Trouble with STEAM and Why We Use It Anyway," *Science Education* 105, no. 2 (2021): 209–231.

4. Mejias et al., "The Trouble with STEAM."

5. Bronwyn Bevan, Kylie Peppler, Mark Rosin, Lynn Scarff, Elisabeth Soep, and Jen Wong, "Purposeful Pursuits: Leveraging the Epistemic Practices of the Arts and Sciences," *Converting STEM into STEAM Programs: Methods and Examples from and for Education* (2019): 21–38.

6. Maxine Greene, *Releasing the Imagination: Essays on Education, the Arts, and Social Change* (San Francisco: Jossey-Bass Publishers, 1995); bell hooks, "Theory as Liberatory Practice," *Yale Journal of Law and Feminism* 4 (1991): 1–12.

7. Henry Jenkins, Gabriel Peters-Lazaro, and Sangita Shresthova, eds., *Popular Culture and the Civic Imagination: Case Studies of Creative Social Change* (New York: NYU Press, 2019).

8. Shawn A. Ginwright, *Hope and Healing in Urban Education: How Urban Activists and Teachers Are Reclaiming Matters of the Heart* (New York: Routledge, 2015).

9. "Creative Expression," *Gratefulness*, accessed November 18, 2021, https://gratefulness.org/area-of-interest/creative-expression/.

10. Parts of this section and, below, "Erase Your Face" appear in Clifford H. Lee, Nimah Gobir, Alex Gurn, and Elisabeth Soep, "In the Black Mirror: Youth Investigations into Artificial Intelligence," *ACM Transactions on Computing Education*, 2022, http://dx.doi.org /10.1145/3484495; Clifford Lee, Elisabeth Soep, and Nimah Gobir, "Illuminating the Black Mirror: Humanizing Ethics within Artificial Intelligence" (presented at the annual meeting of the American Education Research Association, online post, April 9, 2021). We want to acknowledge our colleagues Nimah Gobir and Alex Gurn for their crucial fieldwork and insights.

11. Inioluwa Deborah Raji, Timnit Gebru, Margaret Mitchell, Joy Buolamwini, Joonseok Lee, and Emily Denton, "Saving Face: Investigating the Ethical Concerns of Facial Recognition Auditing," in *Proceedings of the AAAI/ACM Conference on AI, Ethics, and Society* (New York: Association for Computing Machinery, 2020), 145–151, https://doi.org/10 .1145/3375627.3375820.

12. Ginwright, *Hope and Healing in Urban Education*.

13. Lee, Soep, and Gobir, "Illuminating the Black Mirror."

14. Marjerrie Masicat, "Your Guide to Anti-Surveillance Fashion," YR Media, December 18, 2019, https://yr.media/tech/guide-to-anti -surveillance-fashion/.

15. Joy Buolamwini and Timnit Gebru, "Gender Shades: Intersectional Accuracy Disparities in Commercial Gender Classification," in *Proceedings of Machine Learning Research* 81 (2018): 1–15, https:// proceedings.mlr.press/v81/buolamwini18a/buolamwini18a.pdf.

16. "Five Big Ideas in Artificial Intelligence," accessed November 19, 2021, file:///Users/lissasoep/Downloads/AI4K12_Five_Big_Ideas_Poster .pdf; Duri Long and Brian Magerko, "What Is AI Literacy? Competencies and Design Considerations," in *Proceedings of the 2020 CHI Conference on Human Factors in Computing Systems* (New York: Association for Computing Machinery, 2020), 1–16, https://doi.org/10.1145 /3313831.3376727; Grzegorz Ptaszek, "From Algorithmic Surveillance to Algorithmic Awareness: Media Education in the Context of New

Media Economics and Invisible Technologies," in *Media Education as a Challenge*, ed. Sławomir Ratajski (Warsaw: Academy of Fine Arts in Warsaw, 2020), 59–71; "Learning about Artificial Intelligence: A Hub of MIT Resources for K–12 Students," MIT Media Lab, accessed November 19, 2021, https://www.media.mit.edu/articles/learning -about-artificial-intelligence-a-hub-of-mit-resources-for-k-12-students/; David Touretzky, Christina Gardner-McCune, Fred Martin, and Deborah Seehorn, "Envisioning AI for K–12: What Should Every Child Know about AI?," in *Proceedings of the AAAI Conference on Artificial Intelligence* 33, no. 1 (2019): 9795–9799; Grzegorz Ptaszek, "Media Education 3.0? How Big Data, Algorithms, and AI Redefine Media Education," *Handbook of Media Education Research* (2020): 229–240.

17. Quoted in Elisabeth Soep, Clifford Lee, Sarah Van Wart, and Tapan S. Parikh, "Code for What?: Programming Civic Imagination," in *Popular Culture and the Civic Imagination: Case Studies of Creative Social Change*, ed. Henry Jenkins, Sangita Shresthova, and Gabriel Peters-Lazaro (New York: NYU Press, 2019).

18. Xion Abiodun, Valeria Araujo, Victoria Balla, Zoe Harwood, Dante Ruberto, Bayani Salgado, Ariel Tang, et al., "Erase Your Face," YR Media, October 20, 2020, https://interactive.yr.media/erase-your-face/.

Chapter 7

1. C. Richard Snyder, "Hope Theory: Rainbows in the Mind," *Psychological Inquiry* 13, no. 4 (2002): 249–275.

2. "Comparison with CSP Framework," Beauty and Joy in Computing, accessed March 14, 2021, https://bjc.edc.org/June2020bjc2/bjc-r/cur /compare.html.

3. Dawn Royal and Art Swift, "U.S. Minority Students Less Exposed to Computer Science," Gallup, October 18, 2016, https://news.gallup.com /poll/196307/minority-students-less-exposed-to-computer-science.aspx.

4. Ruha Benjamin, Troy Duster, Ron Eglash, Nettrice Gaskins, Anthony Ryan Hatch, Andrea Miller, Alondra Nelson et al., *Captivating Technology* (Durham, NC: Duke University Press, 2019), 14.

5. Alondra Nelson, "Introduction: Future Texts," *Social Text* 20, no. 2 (2002): 1–15.

6. Bettina L. Love, *We Want to Do More than Survive: Abolitionist Teaching and the Pursuit of Educational Freedom* (Boston: Beacon Press, 2019).

7. Angela Calabrese Barton and Edna Tan, "Designing for Rightful Presence in STEM: The Role of Making Present Practices," *Journal of the Learning Sciences* 28, no. 4–5 (October 20, 2019): 616–658, https://doi.org/10.1080/10508406.2019.1591411; Ayana Allen-Handy, Valerie Ifill, Raja Y. Schaar, Michelle Rogers, and Monique Woodard, "Black Girls STEAMing through Dance: Inspiring STEAM Literacies, STEAM Identities, and Positive Self-Concept," in *Challenges and Opportunities for Transforming from STEM to STEAM Education*, ed. Kelli Thomas and Douglas Huffman (Hershey, PA: IGI Global, 2020), 198–220; Mia Shaw and Yasmin Kafai, "Restorying as Critical Praxis: Reimagining Dominant Narratives through Computational Quilts" (paper presented at the International Computing Education Research Conference, New Zealand, August 10–12, 2020).

8. "A Glossary of Pali and Buddhist Terms," accessed November 19, 2021, https://www.accesstoinsight.org/glossary.html#m; Sharon Salzberg, *Lovingkindness: The Revolutionary Art of Happiness* (Boston: Shambhala, 2002).

9. Shawn Ginwright, "The Future of Healing: Shifting from Trauma-Informed Care to Healing-Centered Engagement," *Medium*, May 31, 2018, https://ginwright.medium.com/the-future-of-healing-shifting-from-trauma-informed-care-to-healing-centered-engagement-634f557ce69c.

10. Elizabeth Alexander, "'We Must Be about Our Father's Business': Anna Julia Cooper and the In-Corporation of the Nineteenth-Century African-American Woman Intellectual," *Signs: Journal of Women in Culture and Society* 20, no. 2 (January 1995): 336–356, https://doi.org/10.1086/494977.

11. Joel H. Spring, *Deculturalization and the Struggle for Equality: A Brief History of the Education of Dominated Cultures in the United States* (New York: Routledge, 2016); Tara J. Yosso, "Whose Culture Has Capital? A

Critical Race Theory Discussion of Community Cultural Wealth," *Race Ethnicity and Education* 8, no. 1 (March 2005): 69–91, https://doi.org/10.1080/1361332052000341006.

12. Myles Horton and Paulo Freire, *We Make the Road by Walking: Conversations on Education and Social Change* (Philadelphia: Temple University Press, 1990).

13. *We Literally Redrew Our Community (and You Can Too)*, YR Media, December 3, 2018, https://yr.media/identity/jersey-city-gentrification -illustrated-teens/.

14. "The Jax," accessed November 19, 2021, https://thejax.online /about-us (site discontinued).

15. "What Is the Civic Imagination?," Civic Imagination Project, accessed November 19, 2019, https://www.civicimaginationproject .org/; Henry Jenkins, Gabriel Peters-Lazaro, and Sangita Shreshtova, eds., *Popular Culture and the Civic Imagination: Case Studies of Creative Social Change* (New York: NYU Press, 2020).

16. Nicole Mirra and Antero Garcia, "'I Hesitate but I Do Have Hope': Youth Speculative Civic Literacies for Troubled Times," *Harvard Educational Review* 90, no. 2 (June 1, 2020): 295–321, https://doi.org/10 .17763/1943-5045-90.2.295.

17. Yosso, "Whose Culture Has Capital?"

18. Ginwright, "The Future of Healing"; C. R. Snyder, Shane J. Lopez, Hal S. Shorey, Kevin L. Rand, and David B. Feldman, "Hope Theory, Measurements, and Applications to School Psychology," *School Psychology Quarterly* 18, no. 2 (2003): 122–139, https://doi.org/10.1521/scpq.18 .2.122.21854.

19. Henry Jenkins, Sangita Shreshtova, Liana Gamber-Thompson, Neta Kligler-Vilenchik, and Arely Zimmerman, *By Any Media Necessary: The New Youth Activism* (New York: NYU Press, 2016).

20. Desmond Meagley and Youth Radio, "They/Them Pronouns: All Your Questions about Gender Neutral Pronouns Answered," *TeenVogue*, December 15, 2021, https://www.teenvogue.com/story/they-them -questions-answered.

21. Desmond Meagley, Jen Tribbet, Peter Disney, and Paulina Ortega, "In Their Own Words: Beyond the Binary," YR Media, June 20, 2018, https://yr.media/identity/in-their-own-words-beyond-the-binary/. All quotes in the following paragraphs are from this piece.

Chapter 8

1. For several of the interactives described in this book, we have packaged the source code for you to remix and repurpose in your own projects: https://yr.media/category/interactive/.

2. D'Artagnan Scorza, Melanie Bertrand, Mark A. Bautista, Ernest Morrell, and Corey Matthews, "The Dual Pedagogy of YPAR: Teaching Students and Students as Teachers," *Review of Education, Pedagogy, and Cultural Studies* 39, no. 2 (March 15, 2017): 139–160, https://doi.org/10.1080/10714413.2017.1296279.

3. "Land Acknowledgement," Code for Anchorage, accessed November 19, 2021, https://land.codeforanchorage.org/; Native Land Digital, accessed November 19, 2021, https://native-land.ca/; Anchorage iTeam, accessed November 19, 2021, https://medium.com/anchorage-i-team.

4. Jasmine Kabatay and Rhiannon Johnson, "Charting Progress on Indigenous Content in School Curricula," CBC News, October 2, 2019, https://www.cbc.ca/news/indigenous/indigenous-content-school-curriculums-trc-1.5300580.

5. Robert Jagers, Deborah Rivas-Drake, and Teresa Borowski, "Equity and Social and Emotional Learning: A Cultural Analysis," *Frameworks Briefs* (November 2018), 1–17.

6. "English Language Arts Standards Grade 9–10," Common Core, accessed November 19, 2019, http://www.corestandards.org/ELA-Literacy/W/9-10/.

7. "App Building Guides," MIT App Inventor, accessed November 19, 2021, https://appinventor.mit.edu/explore/app-building-guides.

8. Amanda Agustin, "What It's Like to Be a Translator," YR Media, July 24, 2016, https://yr.media/news/what-its-like-to-be-a-translator/.

9. "YR Toolkit," MIT App Inventor, accessed November 19, 2021, http://ai2.appinventor.mit.edu/?locale=en&repo=http%3A%2F%2Fappinventor.mit.edu%2Fyrtoolkit%2Fyr%2FaiaFiles%2Fhello_bonjour%2Ftranslate_tutorial.asc#5570195877134336.

10. "Only Smiling on the Outside: Teens Hide Depression," YR Media, March 23, 2016, https://yr.media/news/only-smiling-on-the-outside-teens-hide-depression/.

11. Ajani Torres-Cedillo, "Could Your Next Therapist Be Your Phone?," YR Media, May 1, 2017, https://yr.media/news/could-your-next-therapist-be-your-phone/.

12. Mike Tissenbaum, Josh Sheldon, and Hal Abelson, "From Computational Thinking to Computational Action," *Communications of the ACM* 62, no. 3 (February 21, 2019): 34–36, https://doi.org/10.1145/3265747.

13. *Facemesh Filter Camera*, MIT App Inventor, accessed November 19, 2021, https://appinventor.mit.edu/explore/resources/ai/facemesh.

14. "Using the MIT App Inventor FaceExtension (for Facemesh)," *Sparse-Dense*, accessed November 19, 2021, https://sparse-dense.blogspot.com/2021/03/using-mit-app-inventor-faceextension.html.

15. "Awesome Dancing with AI Tutorial," *Sparse-Dense*, accessed November 19, 2021, https://sparse-dense.blogspot.com/2021/01/awesome-dancing-with-ai-tutorial.html.

16. Ruha Benjamin, *Race after Technology: Abolitionist Tools for the New Jim Code* (Medford, MA: Polity Press, 2019).

17. Joy Buolamwini and Timnit Gebru, "Gender Shades: Intersectional Accuracy Disparities in Commercial Gender Classification," in *Proceedings of Machine Learning Research* 81 (2018): 1–15, https://proceedings.mlr.press/v81/buolamwini18a/buolamwini18a.pdf.

18. "Posenet," accessed May 15, 2021, https://ml5js.org/reference/api-PoseNet/.

19. Robinson Meyer, "The Repeat Racism of Snapchat," *Atlantic*, August 13, 2016, https://www.theatlantic.com/technology/archive

/2016/08/snapchat-makes-another-racist-misstep/495701/; Sara Li, "The Problems with Instagram's Most Popular Beauty Filters, from Augmentation to Eurocentrism," *Nylon*, October 7, 2020, https:// www.nylon.com/beauty/instagrams-beauty-filters-perpetuate-the -industrys-ongoing-racism.

20. Oakland Museum of California, accessed November 19, 2021, https://museumca.org/about-omca?qt-mission_history_central=1 #qt-mission_history_central.

21. "Oakland, I Want You to Know . . . ," Oakland Museum of California, accessed November 19, 2021, https://museumca.org/exhibit/oak land-i-want-you-to-know#:~:text=Oakland%2C%20I%20want%20you %20to%20know%E2%80%A6&text=Experience%20artwork%20that %20asks%20provocative,happening%20throughout%20Oakland %20right%20now.

22. Jeffrey Edalatpour, "OMCA 'Wants You to Know' Your West Oakland Neighbors," KQED, July 26, 2016, https://www.kqed.org/arts/1185 1411/omca-wants-you-to-know-your-west-oakland-neighbors.

23. Cynthia Stone and Joe Matazzoni, "Reframed: Artists Seeking Social Change Bring the Public into the Picture," KQED, April 22, 2015, https://www.kqed.org/arts/10577919/reframed-artists-seeking -social-change-bring-the-public-into-the-picture.

24. Science Gallery Dublin, accessed November 19, 2021, https:// dublin.sciencegallery.com/.

25. "About," Science Gallery Dublin, accessed November 19, 2021, https://sciencegallery.org/about-network.

26. European ARTificial Intelligence Lab, accessed November 19, 2021, https://ars.electronica.art/ailab/en/.

27. "After Hours at Science Gallery Dublin," Science Gallery Dublin, accessed November 19, 2021, https://dublin.sciencegallery.com/events /after-hours-at-science-gallery-dublin.

28. James A. Jaramillo, "Vygotsky's Sociocultural Theory and Contributions to the Development of Constructivist Curricula," *Education* 117, no. 1 (1996): 133–141.

29. Vivian Chávez and Elisabeth Soep, "Youth Radio and the Pedagogy of Collegiality," *Harvard Educational Review* 75, no. 4 (December 1, 2005): 409–434, https://doi.org/10.17763/haer.75.4.827u365446030386.

30. Angela Calabrese Barton and Edna Tan, "Designing for Rightful Presence in STEM: The Role of Making Present Practices," *Journal of the Learning Sciences* 28, no. 4–5 (October 20, 2019): 616–658, https://doi .org/10.1080/10508406.2019.1591411.

Epilogue

1. Victoria Burton-Harris and Philip Mayor, "Wrongfully Arrested Because Face Recognition Can't Tell Black People Apart," ACLU News and Commentary, June 24, 2020, https://www.aclu.org/news/privacy -technology/wrongfully-arrested-because-face-recognition-cant-tell -black-people-apart/.

2. Randy Wimbley and David Komer, "Black Teen Kicked out of Skating Rink after Facial Recognition Camera Misidentified Her," Fox 2 Detroit, July 14, 2021, https://www.fox2detroit.com/news/teen-kicked -out-of-skating-rink-after-facial-recognition-camera-misidentified-her.

3. Jeffrey Dastin, "Amazon Extends Moratorium on Police Use of Facial Recognition Software," Reuters, May 18, 2021, https://www.reuters.com /technology/exclusive-amazon-extends-moratorium-police-use-facial -recognition-software-2021-05-18/.

4. Zoe Harwood and YR Interactive, "Surveillance U: Has Virtual Proctoring Gone Too Far?," YR Media, https://interactive.yr.media/has -virtual-proctoring-gone-too-far/.

Acknowledgments

1. Paulo Freire, *Pedagogy of the Oppressed* (New York: Continuum, 1996).

Index